Using the Sky

In the mid 1990s Deborah Hay's work took a new turn. From her early experiments with untrained dancers, and after a decade of focusing on solo work, the choreographer began to explore new grounds of choreographic notation and transmission by working with experienced performers and choreographers.

Using the Sky: a dance follows a similar path to Hay's previous books – *Lamb at the Altar* and *My Body, the Buddhist* – by chronicling her unrelenting quest for ways to both define and rethink her choreographic imagery through a broad range of alternately intimate, poetic, analytical, and often playful engagement with language and writing.

This book is a reflection on the experiments that Hay set up for herself and her collaborators and the ideas she discovered while choreographing four dances: *A Lecture on the Performance of Beauty* (2003), *If I Sing to You* (2008), *No Time to Fly* (2010), and the solo *my choreographed body* (2014).

The works are revisited by unfolding a trove of notes and journal entries, resulting in a dance score in its own right and providing an insight into Hay's extensive legacy and her profound influence on the current conversations in contemporary performance arts.

Deborah Hay began her career in NYC in the early 1960s. In five decades at the vanguard of choreographic experimentation she has helped redefine the field of dance with her revolutionary work and insightful publications. She is regarded as one of the most influential contemporary choreographers.

Using the Sky

a dance

Deborah Hay

Routledge
Taylor & Francis Group

LONDON AND NEW YORK

First published 2016
by Routledge
2 Park Square, Milton Park, Abingdon, Oxon OX14 4RN

and by Routledge
711 Third Avenue, New York, NY 10017

Routledge is an imprint of the Taylor & Francis Group, an informa business

British Library Cataloguing-in-Publication Data
A catalogue record for this book is available from the British Library

Library of Congress Cataloguing-in-Publication Data
Hay, Deborah, 1941-
Using the sky : a dance / Deborah Hay.
pages cm
1. Modern dance. 2. Choreography. I. Title.
GV1783.H374 2016
792.8—dc23
2015012313

ISBN: 978-1-138-91435-3 (hbk)
ISBN: 978-1-138-91437-7 (pbk)
ISBN: 978-1-315-69087-2 (ebk)

Typeset in Stempel Garamond LT Std
by Swales & Willis Ltd, Exeter, Devon, UK

For Savannah and Ella Jane

Contents

Figures

Preface

February 20, 2013

I am among friends. It is evening and the lake is dark and still. There is a red circular life buoy floating some distance from shore. Drifting on my back, cradled by the buoy, I realize my mind is in a thousand places so I look up at the sky. At first I see only blackness. Soon enough shades of pale amber light reveal layers of shifting and billowing clouds that force my breath to rise. Then I begin to wonder how far I have drifted. Trying to twist around to see land I fear capsizing. I take a moment to decide not to worry, and turn back to the sky.

Acknowledgements

I am indebted to the following dancers, each one an extraordinary test site for my choreography since 2000. The full cast for each ensemble work is listed here, so a few dancers are acknowledged more than once because they appeared in several works. These artists have had a particularly strong impact on the development of my choreography and I would not be where I am now without their sensitivity and passion.

Whizz (2001): Raquel Aedo, Mikhail Baryshnikov, Emily Coates, Rosalynde LeBlanc, Michael Lomeka, Emanuele Phuon, Keith Sabado

Single Duet (2001): Mikhail Baryshnikov

The Match (2004): Wally Cardona, Mark Lorimer, Chrysa Parkinson, Ros Warby

"O, O" (2005 & 2006): (the New York and French adaptations) Jeanine Durning, Neil Greenberg, Miguel Gutierrez, Juliette Mapp, Vicky Schick, and, in France, Nuno Bizarro, Corinne Garcia, Emmanuelle Huynh, Jennifer Lacey, Catherine Legrand, Laurent Pichaud, Sylvain Prunenec

Mountain (2007): Gaelen Hanson, Peggy Piacenza, Amelia Reeber

Grope and Find It and Pull It Out (2008): Andrea Buckley, Rachel Krische, Jane Mason, Fiona Millward

If I Sing to You (2008): Michelle Boulé, Jeanine Durning, Catherine Legrand, Juliette Mapp, Vera Nevanlinna, Amelia Reeber

Up Until Now (2009): Alana Elmer, Mairi Greig, Syreeta Hector, David Houle, Yuichiro Inoue, Pulga Muchochoma, Simon Renaud, Kaitlin Standeven, Brodie Stevenson, Naishi Wang, Sarah Wasik, Linnea Wong

Breaking the Chord (2010): Clara Amaral, Koldo Arostegui, Esther Arribas, Fernando Belfiore, Marlene Bunge, William Collins, Marina Colomina, Nina Djekic, Florentina Holzinger, Setareh Fatehi Irani, Tomislav Feller, Adriano Jensen, Marzena Krzenimska, Lilach Livne, Andriana Lubina, Thibault Maillard, Adrius Mulokas, Magdalena Ptasznik, Alice Pons, Noha Ramadan, Olivia Reschofsky, Vincent Riebeek, Michele Rizzo, Karina Sarkissova, Agata Siniarska, Rodrigo Sobarzo, Alma Soderberg, Eva Susova, Simon Tanguy, Olga Tsvetkova, Lisa Vereertbrugghen, Marta Ziolek, Alexander Gershberg, Sara Ostertag

Lightening (2010): Joona Halonen, Satu Halttunen, Anne Hiekkaranta, Jyrki Karttunen, Jenni-Elina Lehto, Vera Nevanlinna

A Lost Opera (2011): Ella Clarke, Julie Lockett, Cindy Cumming

As Holy Sites Go (2011): Jeanine Durning, Juliette Mapp, Ros Warby

Blues (2012): Rashaun Mitchell, Omagbitse Omagbemi, Samantha Speis, Simone Sobers, April Matthis, Judith Sanchez Ruiz, Malcolm Low, Paul Hamilton, Stacy Spence, Niv Acosta, Marya Wethers, Maggie Jones, Abby Block, Meredith Fages, Kathy Wasik, Margaret Paek, Jocelyn Tobias, Laurie Berg, Emily Moore, Stephanie Miracle, Hana van der Kolk, Rebecca Davis

Richmond Hall (2012): Joanna Friesen, Neil Ellis Orts, Angeles Romero, Leslie Scates, Paul Smith, Toni Valle

As Holy Sites Go/duet (2012): Jeanine Durning and Ros Warby

Not included are the names of more than 300 dancer/choreographers who participated in my annual Solo Performance Commissioning Project from 1998 through 2012. The experience of working with these individuals was way more than one person deserves. I salute them and that book will come.

Since 2000, the consistent administration, production, and/or presentation of my work by several presenters, producers, artists, and educators have been gifts of a lifetime.

Jennifer Tipton

Mikhail Baryshnikov

Bill Forsythe and The Forsythe Company

Michèle Steinwald

Judy Hussie-Taylor, Laurie Uprichard and Danspace Project, in NYC

Movement Research, New York, USA

Gill Clarke and Fiona Millward of Independent Dance, London, England

Kirsi Monni and Raija Ojala of the Theater Academy and Zodiak in Helsinki, Finland

Festival d'Automne, Paris, France

Dancehouse, and Jane Refshauge, Melbourne, Australia

Christopher House and Toronto Dance Theatre, Canada

Gabriel Smeets

L'Atelier de Paris Carolyn Carlson, Vincennes, France

P.A.R.T.S, Brussels, Belgium

Josette Pisani, Danse Objectif, Marseille, France

I am proud and grateful for the insight, encouragement, and support I have received from Scott deLahunta. Along with the input and creativity from Amin Webber and Florian Jenett throughout the Motion Bank project, we were able to take the ball, run with it, and manage to reach home together!

I am deeply appreciative to Laurent Pichaud, who began working with me as a dancer/choreographer and translator in 2006. He has since assisted in several of my commissioned works and other projects. We have grown into real buddies.

I thank my brother, the poet Barry Goldensohn, who edited the first draft of this book, and his wife Lorrie, who lent her expertise to editing the first round of proofs. I am grateful too to the folks at Mad Brook Farm, where

I spent three summer months finishing this manuscript and returning to my solo practice in the living room and on the porch of the main house.

In Austin, TX the Deborah Hay Dance Company Board of Directors stand by me in ways that I believe none of us yet realize. They are Beverly Bajema, Claudia Boles, Anna Carroll, Will Dibrell, Emily Little, Sherry Smith, and Sydney Yeager. My friend Rino Pizzi has been there in friendship, photography, website management, and helping fix things I don't understand. My gratitude also goes to Diana Prechter and Kent Cole, who have helped enhance the DHDC in many logistical ways.

Meeting and working with Talia Rogers, publisher of Routledge Theater and Performance Studies, felt like the launch of a friendship. Everyone at Routledge worked to turn the manuscript into a book in record time. My appreciation and gratitude is profound.

And last but not least are recent grants/awards that have helped free me from the struggle for survival that once shaped the course of every day. I owe profound gratitude to the USA Artists grant in 2010, the 2011 Foundation for Contemporary Arts grant, the Robert Rauschenberg artist's residency program 2014, and most especially the 2012 inaugural Doris Duke Artist's Award Program.

Using the Sky is also the name of my score as it appears on the Motion Bank website.

Notes on the Text

The essay, "My Body, the Archive," was first commissioned by The Pew Center for Arts & Heritage, Philadelphia. © 2014 The Pew Center for Arts & Heritage. All rights reserved.

"A Lecture on the Performance of Beauty" was published in *Choreographic Practices*, Volume 5, Number 1, in 2014.

No Time to Fly was self-published in 2010 in Austin, TX, and in 2013 it was republished *as is* by CasCo, Office for Art, Design and Theory, Utrecht, the Netherlands.

Foreword

Deborah Hay:
Absurdly Coherent Information

The words and ideas contained in this remarkable book by Deborah Hay mark a particular period within her creative practice – 2000 through 2015. With ample wit and wisdom, her nuanced observation illuminates her substantial contribution to dance. Autobiographical in style, *Using the Sky* strikes me as Deborah Hay's most recent self-portrait: it is like the portraiture long used by visual artists as a self-referential record of their practice, where the evolving technique, choice of palette, scale, and materials contain volumes of information for the viewer. The words of Deborah's "self-portrait" move continuously, and her brushstrokes are as intricate as they are wildly generous.

These past fifteen years bracket a prolific body of choreographic creation, where heightened opportunity has broadend the points of access to her work worldwide. The support and involvement of many artists have played defining roles in propelling this trajectory, and it has been a fertile period indeed. Yet as she describes it, this chapter of her work almost didn't arrive.

My own curatorial perspective on Deborah Hay's work comes out of an artist-centered background. I have learned that her singular impact is far-reaching; her use of language one of her uniquely vital tools. The title of this book, *Using the Sky*, I interpret as an invitation.

Whidbey Island (Summer Sky)

My first encounter with Deborah Hay was in August of 1999, where I found myself in an unlikely location to meet one of the originators of Judson Church and the postmodern dance movement that was spawned throughout the downtown dance scene of New York during the 1960s and 1970s. We met on Whidbey Island, in the San Juan Island chain off the coast of Washington State. Deborah was there to run her intensive "Solo Performance Commissioning Project" for a predetermined number of people that had signed on as participants.

I knew one of the participants – the Australian-based dancer and choreographer, whom I had worked with as an artistic director at the Portland Institute for Contemporary Art, and it was through her encouragement that I began to learn about the singular Deborah Hay. She had invited me to see the "showing" that would happen on the final day.

Ros had made the trip from Australia in order to take part. There were many other dancer/mover/performers, similarly coming from far off, like Deborah herself. I pulled into the gravel parking area of the Whidbey Island Center for the Arts, thinking: "Of all the places to hold a dance intensive, how on earth did she pick this one?" This is a place in the Pacific Northwest known mainly for its military base, crab fishing, timber, and rain.

Sitting inconspicuously on the floor, I was among a group of twenty-plus people in their comfortable layers and bare feet, one of the only people watching. The full majority were involved in *doing*. Deborah was readying them in a warm-up while offering what seemed unusual and random instructions. Not being familiar with her working process, I could not make sense of the words that the performers embraced with head nods and full absorption. Hay walked over to welcome me and handed me a short printed program. They would all be performing their solo adaptation of a work entitled *Fire*.

Not only had the performers traveled some distance to arrive at this moment, they came from vastly different performance backgrounds as well. Watching them all perform their "solo adaptation" simultaneously was akin to hearing numerous languages being spoken at once. I knew they were "speaking" from the same text, although the movement itself spun off into radically different results. I could not decipher what was being "said" nor where to place my attention. The experience of the work was as odd as it was captivating.

Driving Ros Warby to the ferry terminal afterwards, I asked her questions about the process I had witnessed. While there had been pattern, shape, and a rich dimensionality, I could not recognize the choreographic system underpinning *Fire*.

New York (Winter Sky)

I saw *Fire* again much later at Dancespace in New York as part of an evening entitled *Boom, Boom, Boom*. This time, Warby and Hay each performed their own adaptation of the material, before an audience of dance practitioners and others active in the downtown art scene, where regular exposure to experimental work is a part of one's daily diet. This *Fire* was a performance where the diligent practice of Deborah Hay and the articulation of Warby bolted forward into a lasting and potent recognition of Deborah's work for everyone there. I saw once more the piece that I had experienced on Whidbey Island, but with heightened resonance. This *Fire* remained perfectly absurd, but left a glorious charge in the air.

In my subsequent discussions with curatorial colleagues, they expressed frustration about the limited access to Deborah's work outside of Dancespace and Movement Research in New York. Deborah was highly esteemed by postmodern dance and practitioners of improvisation, but those running dance presenting organizations nationally had their focus elsewhere.

Deborah was part of PAST/FORWARD, a brilliant survey of the choreographers and artists from Judson Church that Mikhail Baryshnikov had commissioned for the White Oak Dance Company. There was much anticipation at the outset; a healthy touring life and critical acclaim followed. PAST/FORWARD amplified the legacy of the creative research and work of the Judson Church dance scene and, by design, it also brought greater awareness of the artists that had continued to create work these many decades later. As PAST/FORWARD continued to tour the world, Deborah returned to the studio.

I began to realize how Deborah's precisely crafted instructional phrases are woven into a "score." Her scores are remarkable in their own right, and truly "impossible" to execute if one were to assume there is a "right" or "correct" way of yielding a result. Her dances are meant to provoke what she calls a dis-attachment from learned techniques in service to being in the very potential of the performance exactly while it is taking place. It likely goes without saying that this is of great value to performers themselves.

I didn't quite know how to convert this kind of "process-based" information into a curatorial/presenting framework engaging the interests of audiences. How might I enlist audiences to support dance that is not like the dance they think they know, but one that possesses a new singularity and resonance?

In hindsight, I was beginning to ask audiences to do what Deborah Hay was asking performers to do – explore the possible discovery of something exceptional by dis-attaching from what had already been learned through previous experience.

In 2003 Deborah contacted me to revisit an earlier invitation. She was interested in translating her choreographic practice onto "professional dancers," some of whom were also acknowledged choreographers. Her choices to select and invite highly accomplished artists for the work was a marked departure. Rather than perform the piece herself, she would be applying her experimentation and ideas through their individual capacities and technique.

Dancespace had agreed to commission it, and I was more than happy to commit my organization's support early on. The project was called *The Match*.

The dancers whom Deborah had initially envisioned formed the quartet of *The Match*: Ros Warby, Wally Cardona, Chrysa Parkinson, and Mark Lorimer. In 2004 *The Match* premiered at Dancespace, the organization that had long served as Deborah's artistic home in New York City. *The Match* illuminated to beautiful effect her non-linear provocations when placed in collision with the achieved techniques held to by each of the dancers. It was evident that their collective approach ensured that the process itself was as useful to their practice as it was to Deborah's. Through destabilizing/unhinging the experiential structures that these exceptionally proficient bodies had powerfully in place, something sublime and Other emerged for all of them. *The Match* was profoundly expressive, a spectacular moment acknowledging the depth of Hay's practice. After the premiere there was resounding agreement that this was a major work of art. Later that year, Deborah Hay received the 2004 Bessie Award.

Portland, Oregon (Autumn Sky 2004)

I presented the solo adaptations of *The Match* as part of the 2004 Time-based Art Festival at PICA and, as with her premiere in New York, the audiences were riveted. Fortuitously, I was hosting a group of artistic directors and dance curators from France during that year's festival and all were immensely interested in Deborah Hay after they saw the performance. At lunch the next day they excitedly pressed me about where she came from, and how it was possible that they didn't know her work when they knew so much about so many other American choreographers. It occurred to me to compare Deborah Hay to the American painter Georgia O'Keefe, who had also chosen to leave New York and its attendant ambitions for the desert landscapes of the southwest, in order to "be able to work."

Melbourne, Australia (Spring Sky 2008)

I invited Deborah's piece, *If I Sing to You*, to the Melbourne International Arts Festival where I was then serving as the artistic director. By then her work had widely penetrated into Europe, where important dance festivals and artistic directors had invited *The Match* (Montpellier in France/Dance Umbrella in the UK, etc.) and her mobility was increasing. Deborah was now receiving commissions and well-warranted acknowledgement. The circulation of her ideas had broadened and her explorations with exceptional professional dancers had continued to deepen. The project had been commissioned by William Forsythe through his own dance company – another hugely respected artist propelling Deborah's ideas to a larger audience, within a relationship that continues to this day.

If I Sing to You had no music (there would be some vocalizations generated by the dancers into individual spontaneous songs). The lighting was diffused, without dramatic embellishment or color, and the scene design was the stage itself and a white floor surface. The running time was approximately one hour and twenty minutes with no intermission. All of the cues were determined by the movement changes of the performers, which they would decide in situ. The dancers were all female, and they were responsible for selecting either their male or female costume for each performance. Deborah had one rule about costuming: both genders had to be represented onstage and this varied with each performance.

As with *Fire* in New York (and with *The Match* everywhere it went), the audience at the opening night of *If I Sing to You* was palpably rapt. Success was due to the sheer honesty of Deborah's practice remaining utterly on course.

Los Angeles (Spring Sky 2015)

Deborah recently completed a residency here in Los Angeles, through the organization I now run called Center for the Art of Performance at UCLA. Not surprisingly, her interest lies in exploring new language for describing dance itself. Her approach involved the invention of various word games and interactions with artists, dancers, and a more general audience. She was busy with new epiphanies and her experimentation revealed many layers to mine further. I can only anticipate that wherever her new revelations lead, her powers will be formidable in every direction towards which her practice bends.

I recently asked her about her keen interest in language, and she responded:

> What my body can do is limited. This is not a bad thing because how I choreograph frees me from those limitations. Writing is then how I reframe and understand the body through my choreography.

Being freed from limitations is what I have witnessed and experienced in Deborah's entire body of work, which stands as a gift to those who are engaged in her orbit. Deborah is in complete possession of the skills and disposition to up-end restraints - most typically she has set her sights on those restraints from which artists in particular draw. But perhaps all of us more generally can examine the assets of what we have spent years perfecting, illustrating, and maintaining and consider them anew. Perhaps in doing so we can in some way be liberated from the limitations that our own maturing skills unconsciously present to us later on.

Using the Sky is indeed a generous invitation to draw from Deborah's accumulated observations a departure point from what we already know, so that we can arrive in places we may otherwise never have imagined.

Kristy Edmunds

Introduction

I came to appreciate the art of choreography pretty late in my career as a choreographer. It was 2001. I was with my brother watching a video of Ros Warby performing her adaptation of my solo *Fire* when his hand reached out to touch my arm and he said what I was thinking. "That's who you want to work with." Her sympathetic responsiveness to the language I had created to transmit the solo, including her practice of dis-attachment from those very same responses, was astounding. I knew immediately that I wanted to choreograph ensemble work for dancers whose artistic preferences, like Ros's, inclined toward increasingly subtle instances of insight, irreverence, and revelation. I wanted *to choreograph a spoken language* that would inspire a shift in dance away from the illustrative body, despite its intense appeal to dancers and audiences alike, to a non-representational body.

My dance practice continues to seek less stable instances of being and I try to identify those capricious moments through the structure of language, working and reworking that language to best describe the learning taking place in my spewing multi-dimensional reconfiguring non-linear embodiment of potentiality.

It is this absurdly coherent information that feeds my attachment to dis-attaching from the posture of a single coherent person who dances.

Or maybe my attraction to overseeing these infinitesimally brief instances of insight is because, as a choreographer and dancer, it frees me from needing to be creative. The surplus of output from my whole body at once far exceeds any additional input from me. *My work is how I see while dancing.*

Using the Sky: a dance

Everyone is consciously and unconsciously choreographed, by culture, gender, locale, politics, race, job, history, and so on. As a choreographer I am not interested in another movement technique that imposes a stylistic shape to the body but I am fascinated with how a choreography of language, using as few words as possible, can inspire experimentation that expands a dancer's movement resources and performance potential.

How one perceives one's cellular body is a rational, logistic, and analytic conundrum for anyone other than the individual willing to personally experiment with such a body. Creating language that can potentially stimulate sensually meaningful responses from this cellular entity has been the nature of my work for forty-five years. The translation of this feedback has been the core of my teaching, my personal practice, and my experience of performance.

In 2013 I presented a performative talk at the TanzKongress in Düsseldorf, Germany. Although I was on a self-imposed sabbatical that year I accepted this invitation in part because it was where and when the Motion Bank website, also titled *Using the Sky*, was to be released.

To prepare for the TanzKongress I read through all of my dance journals since 2000, selecting passages that could illustrate how my dance language evolved over a period of fifteen years. When that compilation was complete, *Using the Sky: a dance* had taken shape.

≈≈≈≈≈≈≈≈≈≈≈≈≈≈≈≈≈≈≈≈≈

Already drawn on a large white pad elevated on an easel are three separate bodies of information, on three separate sheets of paper, exhibited one at a time. I stand beside the easel and point to my drawing of a horse with a colorful cart pulled along behind it and say something like, "I am the horse. The cart is my research."

I lift the paper, turn it over the top of the pad to reveal a second page.

5 million cells and up – 1970s

50 billion cells – 1980s

800 billion cells – 1990s

50 trillion cells – 2000s

more than a zillion cells – NOW

"The quantification of my research material is based on published data offered to me by students, Deepak Chopra types, friends, and even family." Under my breath but loud enough for people to hear, I remark that the list also illustrates the absurdity of my practice. That sheet of paper is then folded over the top of the pad to reveal a final page.

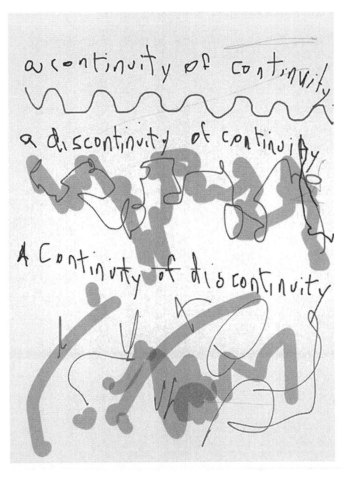

Figure 1 Continuity Drawing (© Deborah Hay, 2014).

a continuity of continuity

a discontinuity of continuity

a continuity of discontinuity

"This is how I describe the evolution of my dance practice as I understand it now."

A continuity of continuity is how those of us who are lucky enough begin life. We are hungry, we are fed. We are thirsty and we drink. We need to be held and are lifted into our mother's arms. We want to dance and we have Fred and Ginger, or hip hop, or B Boys for influence. Or we have ballet. If we want to dance differently, we have modern dance teachers to emulate.

Another example of *a continuity of continuity* is a personal experience of symmetry. Years ago I was performing and teaching as part of a week's residency at Skidmore College. I was invited to observe students from a dance composition class who were making work based on symmetry. *I remember a beauteous feeling of satisfaction that the symmetry evoked as I watched the committed young dancers.* A moment later I realized that my entire career was based on removing anything resembling symmetry from my dances.

I point to the second line of the three listed on the large pad of paper. *A discontinuity of continuity* provides avenues for experimentation that lead to personal insight impossible to realize without risk-taking. It is a necessary step in understanding the power of choice and the recognition of one's limitations. *A discontinuity of continuity* can also be dangerous and I have a great example of that.

About ten years ago I wanted to see if I could unlearn an involuntary action and decided upon sneezing. I never told anyone I was doing this. It wasn't until two years into this experiment that I noticed an annoying itch on the inside corner of my left eye every time I blew my nose. I realized I had ruptured a once secure membrane that was probably created for the sole purpose of preventing nose blowers from subsequent eye itchiness. I am certain the rupture was a direct result of the fairly violent eruptions within my sinus cavity every time a sneeze happened. And, some time later, following a workshop in Brussels where I remember sneezing a lot, I was dining in a fancy airport hotel the evening before returning to Austin. My jaw locked while spooning French onion soup to my mouth. I returned to my room immediately. During the flight home the next day, without much range of movement in my jaw, I panicked, trying to place my head near the retractable tray in order to eat. I immediately went to my dentist to be fitted for a bite guard that eventually caused painful stiffness in my neck. The bite guard was soon in the garbage and with the help of a massage therapist normal jaw activity resumed, along with a commitment to return to my god-given right to sneezing. A dear friend, who never knew about my experiment, recently told me that on some occasions in local restaurants I would sneeze with such appalling sounds and spray that she considered not dining with me again.

Pointing to *a continuity of discontinuity*, I say, "How I arrived here is the context for my talk."

Until the age of twenty-five I held these beliefs about myself:

dance technique was not something I could bring myself to master; my intellect, my thinking mind, was inadequate;

I did not know how, nor was I motivated to engage in research. To this day, I do not know how to use a library.

Ten years later, paralleling the decentralization of my three-dimensional body into a cellular one whenever I danced, I had unintentionally replaced the need to master a way of moving with a body that was now a site for inquiry. Dance became a way for me to learn without thinking, which in turn diminished my fear of not being smart. The attraction to and the determination to keep noticing my cellular body as my teacher showed no sign of weakening. If methodology or attainment were my goals there would be a fundamental absurdity to my research. How could noticing feedback from five million or a zillion cells possibly compute? How would you even do it? Without a technique to master or a predictable outcome to my dancing, the only evidence I had to support my research was the fact that I continued to learn from my practice. And I became a smarter performer, in that there were aggregates of instances within any given performance when I was not governed by learned behavior.

This adaptation of my talk contains excerpts from my dance notes, more or less in chronological order since January 2000. The format conveys how my practice of performance brought me to an understanding of my work as I describe it now, and I point to the continuity of discontinuity material on the easel. There is some repetition because it took years to adapt what I was learning into my daily practice of dance.

"I" reflects notes made after my solo practice. "You" reflects information I wished to remember to transmit to other dancers.

It may help to give an example of what I experience as feedback from my zillion-celled body when I am dancing. "kjdfv hrtrjtwnr litjwhc;rt3;tfkgnu6t ;ejl."

*What is not included in this text is a forty-minute video of dancer/choreographer Jeanine Durning performing an early adaptation of the solo **No Time to Fly**. That video would begin right now, projected on a large screen behind me. There would be just enough volume to hear Jeanine's footsteps and her singing.*

January 2000

What struck me most was how clearly Misha stated that he was a dancer, not a choreographer, and that his work was to serve the choreographer. I would have liked to have had the presence of mind to respond to him by saying that, as the choreographer, how he could best serve me was by feeling served by the choreography.

In 2000 Mikhail Baryshnikov took on another courageous project. Past/Forward was the re-creation of several dances by choreographers associated with Judson Dance Theater in the early sixties, including the commissioning of new works from those choreographers. I choreographed **Single Duet**, *which Misha and I performed during the USA leg of the tour. I did not think that he really ever understood how I worked, yet when I looked at some of the videos of the duet I much prefer watching him. When he would look at me dancing I could see his blue eyes penetrating every detail of my movement and I associated that look with how he learned from his dance teachers as a young boy. He always wanted me to go onstage first because he said that if he could see me, he could then follow.*

The word "served," used by Misha in 2000, became integral to my personal practice in 2014.

Most dance training assumes that there is a single coherent being who dances. My work succeeds when there is no one "one," no single moment, or meaning, movement, image, character, emotion, that exists long enough for either the dancer or audience to identify an "is" that is happening.

If I remove movement as the primary component of dance-making, can the ways I perceive space and time suffice as material within the choreography *and* performance of my work?

> *For many years it was my surrounding space that I perceived changing as I moved. Gradually my experience of perception enlarged to include the whole studio or theater in which I was dancing. This expanded field increased the material available to me as I danced. Why do I need to limit myself to what I am doing in space when I can include my perception of the outer reaches of that space in my dancing? There is nothing abstract in how I experience space and time. On the contrary, I am alert to my whole body's sensual mutability.*

> *How I perceive my bodily experience of time passing is like lying still between the banks of a shallow moving river.*

I set up a proposition in the form of a "what if?" question. The question is meant to inspire and engage the dancer in noticing the sensuality of the feedback from the question as it unfolds in his/her cellular body. The question is not there to be answered. *And*, to not look for an answer requires a lot of work for everyone. That is why the question has to be so attractive for the person who is dancing: " . . . non-knowing is not a form of ignorance but a difficult transcendence of knowledge" (Bachelard, 1994: p. xxii, quoting Jean Lescure, *Lapique*, Galanis, Paris, p. 78).

*The group piece I choreographed for the Past/ Forward Project was titled **Whizz**. The primary question the dancers were to engage in their practice was, "what if every cell in your body at once has the potential to perceive your loyalty to DANCE, and your disinterestedness (in the loyalty) simultaneously?" Disinterestedness referred to loyalty and nothing else. (This question, among other things, helps undermine "the look" of the serious artist.)*

(As Marian Chase Lecturer, I began my talk with an ear-splitting bark for one minute at a podium before an audience at the American Dance Therapy Association in Seattle, Washington, October 2000.)

Woof woof woof woof woof woof woof woof Woof WOOFWOOF Woof Woof woof woof woof WOOF WOOF woof woof woof woof WOOF WOOF woof woof woof woof woof woof WOOF woof woof woof WOOF . . .

Within the art form we call dance, I experiment with words to disrupt, often violently, conscious and unconscious movement behavior. "What if alignment is everywhere?" or "what if where I am is what I need?" or "what if my will is my destiny?"

Barking, too, has had a transforming effect on my career as a choreographer, performer, and teacher. I was influenced by a Dutch actress, one soloist among a class of performance artists who were studying with Marina Abramovic during a conference entitled "The Connected Body" at the School for New Dance Development in

Amsterdam in the early 1990s. The actress presented her work in a stairwell alcove between two floors. I sat on the steps looking down into her shielded glass enclosure. Other people were using the stairwell to pass from one showing to another and some stopped to watch her briefly. I stayed. She was nude, and had the flawless body of a tall, thin, thirty-year-old. When she moved it was on all fours; loping, pacing, stretching, attacking, protecting, watching us, or lying down and panting. At times she stood on hind legs to paw at the walls in protest. She barked, growled, moaned. She was not acting. Her whole body was dog – flesh, bones, essence. I remember thinking that I had never seen "dog" before seeing her "dog."

I have friends who own several Labradors. One early morning during a visit to their home in Louisiana, my ritual cup of coffee in hand, we sat on a patio that opened onto acres of pecan orchard. First he, then she, then both, for more than an hour, threw sticks into the orchard for the three dogs to fetch. The sticks were then wrestled from their dripping jaws only to be thrown into the orchard and fetched again. It was clear that the dogs would not be first to stop playing. I remember thinking that this was the most wretched way to have my morning coffee.

I did not grow up with a dog, so it was almost thirty years into my professional life before I realized I had in fact trained myself to be a good dog in relation to my master/ my body, my teacher.

My devotion to the practice of dance is similar to the Labs' to the game. The Labs' attention is on the master's whole body, the energy being summoned; the force behind the throwing arm, the moment stick leaves hand, and the direction stick is aimed. When I go into the studio my attention is on my whole body in response to a set of conditions I set out to explore in the course of my work that day. I am poised, in a metaphorical sense, at the feet of my body, my teacher. My tongue could as well be hanging from the side of my mouth, dripping signals of readiness to be served by my body through dance.

April 2001

Zen saying: *Being in the moment* is not necessarily a great thing; however, it is all there is. My response to this is that there can be *more* to the moment than simply *being in it*.

"Immensity at work" is your openness to enlarging your experience of movement to include the space in which you are dancing. What if every cell in your body at once has the potential to perceive all of space moving as you move through it? "Immensity is within ourselves. It is attached to a sort of expansion of being that life curbs and caution arrests . . . " (Bachelard, 1994: p. 184)

And what if every cell in your body at once has the potential to perceive time passing? These questions can both enlarge and deepen your experience of *being in the moment*.

How I practice performance stimulates my perceptual activity to such a degree that I no longer rely on my wonderful earthbound body and what it can do.

If I turn from movement as a primary component in making dances, replacing it with how I perceive space and time, will this suffice as the two primary components in my choreography?

August 2001

The question applied to the solo dance *Music* is: What if every cell in your body at once has the potential to perceive your movement as your music? Or, what if you call your movement your music? Not music in a harmonic sense, but how your movement segments uninterrupted time. Would this not make your experience of time personal? Your choice to read your movement as music puts time in your hands.

The question is meant to stimulate and compel you to keep returning to it while you are dancing.

Your perception of time is personal, while your perception of space is temporal.

What if every cell in my body at once has the potential to perceive beauty and surrender beauty, both at once, each and every moment? I cannot think my way into the question. I cannot force my eyes to see beauty and surrender beauty. This would occupy too much time. So I release the question from my mind, which I automatically house in my head, and spread the question down through my zillion-celled body. **That** body, my teacher, fosters instantaneously succinct, sensually insightful instances of how beauty might manifest if I do not hold on to what I think or want it to be.

A Lecture on the Performance of Beauty

In 2002 I was invited by Mary Brady to write an essay about the choreographic process for the inaugural edition of a journal, *Choreographic Encounters*, published in 2003 for the Institute for Choreography and Dance in Cork, Ireland. Instead I submitted the written score for the solo dance *o beautiful. A Lecture on the Performance of Beauty* is an edited, expanded, and performed version of the original written score.

Preset: Two large screens, adjacent and flush, are ten to fifteen feet in front of the audience. A drawing on a large pad sits on an easel to the right of the screens. A horizontal and vertical line divide the drawing into four quadrants numbered counterclockwise, beginning with quadrant one at the lower right. A black marker is in the tray. Standing near the easel, I hold and speak extemporaneously into a corded microphone. In my other hand is a binder with the ten-page text for *A Lecture on the Performance of Beauty*.

The title for my solo dance *o beautiful*, choreographed in 2002, was an appropriation of the first two words of a patriotic American song. I was feeling tremendous resentment and anger toward then President Bush and his administration that was coupled with a sense of personal powerlessness in regard to the crimes perpetrated throughout the world during his term of office. I continue to feel this way in relation to American policy at home and abroad.

My challenge in choreographing *o beautiful* was: if I do not set out to choreograph a dance, will a daily performance of the same set of parameters, over the course of a year, ultimately give birth to a dance? This was my goal, because I did not think I could intentionally create a dance about politics.

Pointing to the line drawing on the pad and using the two intersecting straight lines as a guide, I traced my index finger over, around, and through those two lines again and again, to signify my daily resolve to follow the path that is not yet drawn on the paper. I also described the fundamental question that guided my daily practice for more than a year. "What if every cell in my body at once has the potential to perceive beauty and to surrender beauty simultaneously, each and every moment?" I then joked with audiences, trying to reassure them that I knew the question was unknowable but that at the same time the process of entering into the question was transformative, although I could not say how.

Timeline for A Lecture on the Performance of Beauty

o beautiful was choreographed in 2002. That winter I commissioned Laura Cannon, a young dancer/costumer from Austin, TX, to design an outfit inspired by the film *Blade Runner*. I was distraught by the state of affairs in the world. You will see me performing *o beautiful* in the Blade Runner costume on the left screen a little further into *A Lecture* . . .

January 2003 saw my first public performances of *o beautiful* at Zodiak Center for New Dance in Helsinki, Finland, and later at Skidmore College in Saratoga Springs,

NY. Following these performances I decided against the post-apocalyptic attire because of how it influenced my movement and colored my behavior onstage. I found a simple pair of pale blue linen pants and a matching tailored shirt to wear instead.

My solo practice of *o beautiful* continued through early summer in Austin, where temperatures rose into the 90s. I made a point of not turning on the air conditioner in the studio because I was not paying rent. My arrangement with the proprietor was an exchange of practice space for acknowledging his support in my dance programs and newsletters. The studio was a large room among a suite of smaller massage cubicles above a downtown bicycle shop. One morning I stripped off my clothing and danced. I was an animal dancing and the movement felt naked in the most pristine environment imaginable. Nudity became the costume and on the spot I changed the solo's title to *Beauty*.

The London program, in July 2003, began with my solo *Music*. After intermission, clothed in blue linen, I approached the audience and invited a volunteer to the stage. Speaking quietly, I asked if this young woman would follow me upstage and undress me there before returning to her seat. Like a caring mother she carefully removed, folded, and stacked my garments on the floor. *Beauty* was performed only once, at the Greenwich Dance Agency. It felt perfect and I would not perform it again. *A Lecture on the Performance of Beauty* is what replaced *Beauty*.

I signal the technician to start the video of the London performance of **Beauty**, which is then projected on the right screen. I then begin reading from the text.

Notes for the Performer of Beauty

What if the you who dances is less like a dancer and more like a computational neuroscientist whose research currently defines our understanding of consciousness and normalcy? Some differences between your work as a dancer and that of the computational neuroscientist are:

1. Your laboratory functions best when it is empty, whereas a computational neuroscientist needs, at least, a desk, chair, computer, etc.
2. You are not required to write papers in order to be recognized . . . although I can attest to the fact that it can help your career.
3. As a dancer your discipline is in schooling your body to perform, whereas the scientist disciplines her mind.
4. As a dancer your methodologies do not require exactitude because your experimentation is deliberately measureless.

What if there is a question, applied like a guideline for **Beauty**, a question that functions like the rudder of a small boat heading out to sea at night? The rudder is in the hand of an experienced navigator, just as the question is in the body of the dancer. The rudder keeps the boat on course in the same way that the question guides the dancer. The steering hand on the rudder bar is relaxed and responsive, like the mind of the dancer. The boatman is inseparable from his world: the water, the night sky, wind, and the currents that slap against the surface of his launch. In much the same spirit, the theater is your world, and you attend to your navigation by keeping the question current. It is the question that guides you through the night of **Beauty**. To seek an answer is to narrow the immensity of the question.

You are alone onstage and noticeably different from the person who was alone in the dressing room moments ago. Your body brought you to this stage. Here you shimmer. *What if* shimmering is how you experience time passing? Here and gone, here and gone, here and gone ... with an emphasis on the here in the here and gone. Without words to describe it, *what if* your audience senses these shifting boundaries of your body?

What if, as a counterpart to shimmering, you exercise your skills for undermining the ordinariness of time? As strong as your genetic and bodily response to your inner pulse may actually feel, you operate like a jazz musician, who turns a song into an eclectic reconfiguration of notes and phrases that defy order, subvert the expected, and yet coalesce masterfully. Your experimentation questions automatic or naturally flowing movement; movement shaped by behavioral patterning that flows from all of us like a reservoir of training and acquired tastes that lodge like a fashionable ski resort at the foot of a beautiful mountain in the Rockies or Alps, as the case may be.

The Choreographer's Confession

Stage directions: I drop my manuscript and begin talking to the audience about the political crisis in the US. I describe my inability to articulate my concerns about US policy and I hear only my anger and rage. I am fully aware of how ineffective my arguments are under these conditions. I apologize for my lack of factual information and analysis and end with this remark: "Dance is my form of political activism. It is not how I dance or why I dance. It is that I *dance*."

Choreographer's Question for the Performer of Beauty

What if every cell in your body has the potential to perceive beauty and to surrender beauty, simultaneously, each and every moment?

I signal the projectionist to start the video of *o beautiful* on the left screen and I position myself, with a marker, beside the easel and pad. I hold both microphone and written score in my left hand and will gradually draw the floor pattern for the dance with my right, all the while reading from the written score. It is my intention to 1) get wound up in the microphone cord, 2) adjust my glasses frequently, 3) constantly negotiate holding and reading the manuscript and drawing at the same time, and 4) to sing beautifully.

The italicized phrases in the written score are snippets from several patriotic American songs that I sing in the course of *A Lecture . . .*

The Choreography

Do you relate to the presence of a straight path? It is always there, whether it is followed or not. *What if* your experience of a straight path is a source of real or imagined security, order, clarity, and strength within the construct of **Beauty**? *What if* departing from the path takes into account your revolutionary spirit, providing space for the anarchist, the individualist, the surly, the part of you who enjoys playing the odds, testing the limits? *she's the emblem of, the land I love, the home of the free and the brave* You can leave the path because you know where it is when you want to return. Will you risk leaving the path? Are you serious enough to risk BEING foolish? What do you think of life without foolishness? *What if* what really matters is that you remain doggedly aware of the straight path whether you are on or off of it, getting what you need wherever you choose to be? *let freedom ring What if* being off the path yet free of obstinacy or willfulness is an opportunity for change, nuance, absurdity, beauty, inclusion? *my country tis of thee, sweet land of liberty, of thee I sing* The world flowers when you depart from the straight path because leaving it heightens your sense of just where it is. What if a real and/or imagined straight path is the only measure by which you know where you are? The path is your bearing. And, *what if* your choice to perceive and surrender beauty as life unfolds each and every moment, whether you are on the path, or off the path, is your only *means* of survival? *O beautiful, for spacious skies*

At the far end of the straight path, in quadrant one, you begin a counterclockwise journey along a single curve, like the outline of a pregnant belly. *stand beside her, and guide her, through the night with the light from above* What if **Beauty** is the innate performance of feminine power, before memory, without signification, inclusive of emotion? Pure, like a dog with a snake in its jaws, a gorgeous management of energy. *What if*, upon meeting the staged and metaphorical straight path once more, you perceive yourself getting everything you need or think you need? What do you need? The answer is too long, prohibitive, complex. *What if* where I am, wherever I am is what I need? *What if* time is of no consequence? *glory glory halleluja, glory glory halleluja*

In quadrant two, **Beauty** is "work," symbolized by repetitive and insistent movement, driven by your passion to survive, a determination to exist for another year, no matter what. At some point you even get down on the floor with no intention of making this look good. You are determined to experience **Beauty** wherever you are, deliberately avoiding smooth action, alignment, right movement. You do not make it easy or find solutions just because you are performing in front of an audience. You are unbeguiling, caught in making your work work. You are a rat. You will not be misled by looking for beauty in shape and/or content. You notice beauty for infinitesimally small instances. It is gorgeous. It is enough. *o'er the land of the free and the home of the brave*

What if, upon coming up to the straight path once more, you imagine getting everything you need or think you need, like silence in the middle of the day, a scarf in cold weather, cream for your coffee. *every heart beats true*

In the fourth quadrant you lift your head upwards.

Choreographer's aside: Looking upwards can sink a performer. When the head tilts upward, it is as if the connection between the mind and body is severed. As a theatrical gesture the poetic or narrative relevance of "looking up" is not applicable in **Beauty**. For instance, looking up suggests hope and hope has no context onstage except as a function of narrative. Your challenge is to look up in order to enlarge your perception of beauty. *O beautiful, o beautiful*

As you look up you follow a curved path leading to the top of quadrant four, returning to the starting point of **Beauty**, the imagined apex of the dance, the highest point, the holiest of holy places. *my home sweet home, my home sweet home*

Travelling slowly and solemnly downstage, you complete an elongated petal-shaped path. This passage is the resolution of the dance, where you test your affinity for and disconnectedness from the blueprint that has held you in performance. *O beautiful . . . o beautiful*

You then detach from the *blueprint* for **Beauty**, the cipher you have milked for continuity and definition. Entering an imagined void, your wit, pathos, memory, disillusionment, love, and anger, form, and formlessness merge into nothing but **Beauty**.

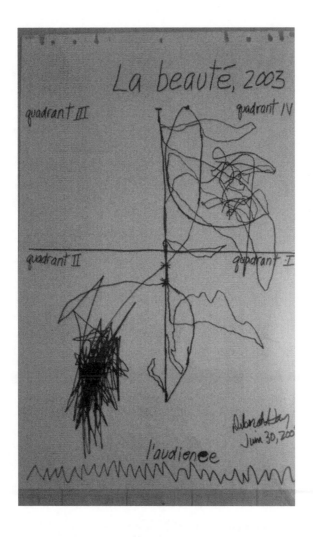

Figure 2 Beauty–Montpellier. Drawing made in Montpellier, France during *A Lecture on the Performance of Beauty* (© Deborah Hay, 2005).

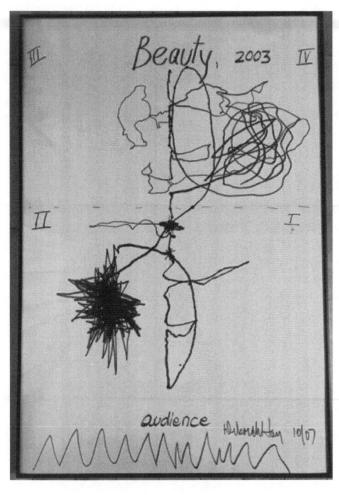

Figure 3 Beauty–Toronto. Drawing made in Toronto, Canada
during *A Lecture on the Performance of Beauty*
(© Deborah Hay 2007).

My actual movement directions are mostly impossible to realize: e.g. cross stage turning without turning. The material can also be embarrassing to do or idiotic to contemplate: e.g. sing a spontaneous patriotic song in a fake language. Or a description can be maddeningly simple: e.g. move along a real or imagined straight path. My movement directions are meant to undermine the response mechanism that leads all of us, including myself, to want to get it right.

January 2002

My perception of space being displaced within a room where I am dancing produces a smooth and fluid sense of tangible perceptual activity. But when I add the word "unique" to my experience of space, because all the moving particles of space and all the moving atoms in my body are irreplaceable, a heightened interest, like a higher gear, engages me in noticing where I am before where I am is gone. Equally, my perception of time passing is vivified by substituting the word "original" for my experience of *here* before *here* is gone.

"What if every cell in your body at once has the potential to perceive the uniqueness and originality of all there is?" "Unique" and "original" are the poetic counterparts of space and time and that inspires me.

> *This was the primary question applied by the cast in the choreography of* **The Match**, *2004.*

This morning my practice revolved around my perception of space as time was passing but it wasn't until I remembered my perception of space as "unique" and my perception of time as "original" that I experienced a genuine joy in dancing.

In 2002 I wrote a letter of resignation to the world of dance that was mailed to about eight presenters/ producers. I felt exhausted after forty years of living in a survival mode as an independent choreographer in the USA. About every seven to ten years I would go about a similar ritual but this was the first time I made it public with other than a few close friends. I went so far as to fill out an application for work at Miller Blueprint, a locally owned art supply store in Austin, TX. But there was one more project I wanted to complete before leaving dance and that was to choreograph an ensemble work for Wally Cardona, Mark Lorimer, Chrysa Parkinson, and Ros Warby. Danspace Project at St. Mark's Church in-the-Bowery commissioned and presented the quartet in 2004 and this "last" dance changed the course of my career.

My standard for success is when a choreographer no longer spends an inordinate amount of energy looking for opportunities to perform. Instead presenters find the choreographers they think will impact their audiences. This happened with **The Match** *and I believe its success was because audiences were able to distinguish the relevancy of my choreography through the artistry of these four superlative dancers. My work was finally seen as not simply idiosyncratic, a word often used in reviews of my solo dances.*

In 2005 the Festival of Dance in Montpellier, France, presented **The Match**. *Merce Cunningham was the featured choreographer in the festival that year and we were paired in a public interview within a teacher/student framework. Merce's influence on my choreography was ignited by his use of time and space, although I do not ever remember him referring to time and space in my four years of study with him. Yet these two elements are what electrified the stage as I watched his company perform and they were attributes of dance that I had never before recognized. During our interview I mentioned the profound effect that his use of time and space had on me and added that I went on to realize the sensuality attributable to each. Merce smiled in response.*

It is possible to remove the angst from the desire to create original and unique movement if you understand that "original" and "unique" pertain to how you perceive your moving body in time and space rather than to what movement you are making with the body.

May 2003

When I *notice* my whole body there is a sense of weightlessness to my experience. I imagine the brevity of a single note to describe how I notice, a buoyancy that lands nowhere. In contrast, *focusing* on my body feels dense. It draws my attention inwards, making it cumbersome to focus elsewhere when the choice arises. It is as if focusing is bound by time and space and noticing is not.

January 2004

When I am dancing I often forget that each moment passing is original. "HERE and gone . . . HERE and gone . . . HERE and gone."

My perception of time passing heightens my sense of here before it is gone.

I need a variable and constant sense of space to counterbalance my attention to time because it is too easy to get seduced by the sensuality of time passing.

To halt your progress through the dance you remain positionless at the threshold of each change in order to surrender behavior that drives you forward onto the next movement. The trick is to remove your innate timing from the sequence of movement directions.

What if "your" consciousness is in direct proportion to the space between where you are dancing in relation to the audience?

The solo *Room* is performed in the round. There is no single area that is front. Or, to quote the dancer Layard Thompson, who learned *Room*, "What if front is everywhere?" You continually choose to surrender the habit of locating yourself in relation to a single direction.

I chose to choreograph **Room** *because I noticed my pattern of creating a front whenever and wherever I was dancing. I found it really idiotic to be in a studio alone and assign front to a blank wall. It wasn't long before I realized that many performers operate similarly. We have learned front, back, right, left,* *and the diagonals that run from corner to corner of a studio or stage. The spaces between those cardinal points have been eliminated from use. The practice of* **Room** *became my remedy for re-establishing contact with the full potential of my visual field.*

Room enlarges your practice of performance by including your perception of the whole room in which you are dancing.

February 2004

The questions are meant to expand how you perceive rather than fix on what you are doing.

June 2004

What if *this theater* is the laboratory and your body is the site where the experiment takes place within the laboratory? What if the question is the material used in the experiment? In order for the experiment to continue it needs the material to support it. Your work as the dancer is to notice the experiment unfolding; how the arousal stimulated by the question changes and informs you. At the same time your perception of the laboratory is necessary to keep you from dwelling on any single aspect of the experiment.

What if every cell in your body at once has the potential to perceive time passing?

The actual floor plan in my solo *The Ridge* is so comforting to *have* that my perception of the uniqueness and originality of all there is must be attended to with greater and greater diligence in order to divert my tendency to *follow* the spatial pattern for the dance.

> *My dances rely on the persistent presence of a question, rendering useless the dependence on memory and anticipation. Instead of action going forward, it is as if it collapses into the moment. The rigor is for the dancer to persistently renew his/her questions rather than conform to the dance's guidelines.*

January 2005

I thought I was watching a play while looking at a video of *The Match* from its Danspace Project, NYC, premiere in February 2004. So I wrote a script for four actors based on the video of the dance. The script contained a description of each dancer's movements transposed to each of the actors. I suggested to the Rude Mechs, a fantastic experimental theatre company based in Austin, TX, that they write a text for the four characters who would have my ready-made movement and staging directions.

> The way I remember it is: You invited us to your house. We all, all rude mechs and you, watched the DVD of the dance with no idea that you were going to ask anything more of us . . . and after it was over you asked us if we would be interested in adapting it to a play . . . and then, because we don't make collective decisions publicly, we left your house, immediately agreed that it was a great idea/opportunity,

and then knocked on your door thirty seconds after we left and said yes . . . I don't think we had seen the dance in Austin yet. (Kirk Lynn)

The Match

A movement script: Deborah Hay

Note that the following text is entirely influenced by the video of the dance *The Match*. A score for the dance was never fully completed. *Match-Play* was created and performed from September 15 to October 15, 2005, at *The Off Center*, in Austin, TX, by Rude Mechs' co-producing artistic directors Lana Lesley, Kirk Lynn, and Shawn Sides and guest artist Barney O'Hanlon of the renowned SITI Company.

The Match has four players.

Note: it is possible to remove the tyranny of having to create original and unique movement if the performer understands that original and unique pertains to how one perceives rather than what one perceives.

Suitable definitions for *The Match*:

1. A person or thing that equals or resembles another in some respect.
2. A person or thing that is an exact counterpart of another.
3. One able to cope with another as an equal.
4. A corresponding or suitably associated pair.
5. A contest or game.

Glossary of sounds performed in respective order in *The Match:*

1. An intermittent spontaneous song, hummed softly.
2. A quietly spoken, untranslatable conversation, with silences.
3. A golf crowd's affirmation, as heard on TV: first the humming of group approval, followed by its applause recreated by smacking the tongue and lips together.
4. The dull thwack of a performer's hands meeting, without clapping.
5. An audible bastardization of #3.
6. "**Fffft**," produced by compressing and widening the lips and using the tongue to catapult the breath out between the front teeth (the mouth's shape quickly restores to keep the source unseen).
7. A complex, non-translatable whispered rhythmic ditty.
8. Two different single syllable sound(s), or word(s), inspired by a cheer heard at a boxing, a tennis, or another kind of match.
9. Blowing out and sucking in air at the same time.
10. An American high school cheering rhythm, 1–2–3, 1–2–3, 1–2–3–4–5–6–7, etc., chanted with a cheerleader's verve, transformed through a spontaneous substitution of single-syllable utterances for each beat.
11. The above ardent single-syllable chant, deconstructed while leaving the mouth.
12. "**Tcct**," a shortened version of "tic."

13. A subdued, unintelligible throaty talking pattern, simultaneously retracted.
14. A single quiet note produced by combining a high and low tone.
15. Spunky illustrative children's-toy utterance(s).

The cast

Cathy

Frank

Charles

Fiona

Time

Under one hour.

Preset

Just before the last few audience members are seated, **Cathy** *enters, performing a simple traveling movement with unflagging buoyancy and rhythm.*

Six minutes later the lights begin to dim.

ACT I

Fiona, Frank, Charles: Enter at their own pace for just a few moments before the lights go out.

In the dark, **Charles, Fiona,** *and* **Frank** *move to a preset position while* **Cathy** *exits.*

Lights

Fi, Fra, Chas: cross to a new location performing smartly executed movement, based on the six-minute rhythmic dance established by **Cathy**. **Fiona** performs center stage.

Note: Smartly executed movement is not driven by inner rhythm, a sense of flow, or a history of training; movement that does not feel personally gratifying.

Fra, Fi, Chas: Like three matches extinguished, movement stops.

Chas: Restart and exit, performing smartly executed movement.

Fi, Fra: Proceed to the next location, performing instances of weightless, lyrical spiraling movements not unlike smoke, but not like it either. Softly hum an intermittent spontaneous love song.

Ca: As **Frank** reaches stage right, step onstage and embrace him.

Fi: Simultaneous with the embrace, become still.

*Note: They embrace upstage and **Fiona's** single figure downstage are as if captured by a long pause.*

Ca, Fra: Simultaneously break into a traveling movement dialogue, with and without physical contact, and a quietly spoken, untranslatable substitute for a real conversation, with silences.

Fi: Simultaneously follow a curved path upstage, inspired by the sounds from the duet.

Chas: Step onstage to form a diagonal line with the others.

Chas, Fi, Fra, Ca: Take one step left.

Blackout

Fra, Ca, Fi, Chas: In the dark take one step right.

Lights

Ca, Chas, Fra, Fi: Perform individual movements, best described as deliberately inconsequential, in close range to one another, eventually recombining into a set formation. Check to see that everyone ends facing the same direction.

Fi, Fra, Chas, Ca: Head turns to look stage left. Produce two different sounds, although they cannot be verified as such: first, a golf crowd's affirmation, as heard on television, humming group approval, followed by its applause, recreated by smacking the tongue and lips together.

Ca, Chas, Fra, Fi: Bend over or somehow lower by half, moving quickly, with deliberate inconsequentiality, maintaining a messy cluster. Produce a sporadic *thwack* from a pair of hands meeting, without clapping. New positions are taken.

Chas, Fra, Fi, Ca: Straighten up, check for identical facing, and turn head stage left. Long pause.

Chas, Fra, Fi, Ca: Television golf sounds repeat.

Ca, Fi, Chas, Fra: Cross stage, as a unit, in one of four roles:

1. A scientist busy at work in the lab,
2. The lab,
3. Someone who undoes the scientist's work,
4. One who oversees the whole shebang.

End in another preset arrangement.

Chas, Ca, Fi, Fra: Heads turn stage left. Short pause. Produce an audible bastardization of the golf audience instructions.

Chas, Ca, Fi, Fra: Follow a curved path upstage, pulled by unrecognizable magnetic forces.

Ca, Fi, Fra, Chas: Choose the sequence for performing three movements:

1. The right lower arm drops quickly, like an ax,
2. Slavishly turn backward and around, and,
3. Without paralleling either #1 or #2, produce a "**fffft**," by compressing and widening the lips and using the tongue to catapult the breath out between the front teeth. Restore the mouth quickly so that the sound's source is unseen.

Fra, Fi, Chas, Ca: Four spontaneous individual rhythmic combinations of snappily executed steps and jumps repeating and traveling along a curved path. Side by side, face inside the curve. Then, fall into a void.

Fi, Chas, Ca, Fra: Retrace path, repeating the same rhythmic combination as before, but face the convex plane of the curve. (The audible rhythmic counterpoint among the four separate combinations is music.)

Ca, Fi, Chas, Fra: Disperse by continuing but distorting the former rhythm and movement.

Fra, Ca, Fi, Chas: Choose sequence to perform three movements:

1. The right arm, bent at the elbow, pokes forward in space.
2. One slavish turn backward and around, and,

3.   Produce, without paralleling either #1 or #2, a "**fffft**," by compressing and widening the lips and using the tongue to catapult the breath out between the front teeth. Restore the mouth quickly so the sound's source is unseen.

Fra, Fi, Ca, Chas: Rather weightless and with little impulse, perform the same movement and rhythm on tippy-toe, drawing stage right to a new set place. Add voice, in a corresponding complex non-translatable whisper, to accompany the elevated footsteps.

Ca, Fi: Produce inconsistently two different single syllable sound(s), or word(s), inspired by a cheer heard at a boxing, a tennis, or another kind of match. Enthusiastically gesture, intermittently. Gradually diminish volume.

Fra, Chas: Run in place. Give no attention to the cheering.

Fra, Fi, Chas, Ca: Cease all action. Lower heads.

Several immediate choices are made and remade:

1.   An exhale matches the force of an inhale as a pair of facing palms exhibit excitement,
2.   Facing hands raise incrementally, sometimes together or separately,
3.   Use odd quick travel to move the action through space, and,
4.   Seemingly important little matches are made.

Chas, Ca, Fi, Fra: Before hands are fully overhead, click fingers, rock body sensually, enjoyably, commandingly, jazzily. (Practice keeps this from schlock.)

Ca, Fi, Fra, Chas: Form a line downstage in front of the audience and break into the all-American high school chanting beat, 1–2–3, 1–2–3, 1–2–3–4–5–6–7, etc. Spontaneously verbalize as single-syllable utterances that cheer each other and the audience. Physically charge the chanting.

Fi, Chas, Ca, Fra: Move backward upstage while the clarity of the single syllables transforms into gobbledygook.

ACT II

Ca, Fi, Fra: One softly spoken linear sentence is cut short with the sound "**tcct**" (short for "tic") and a spontaneous, brief highly stylized dance. Each "**tcct**" starts a new dance, dynamically matching the preceding one but stylistically different from "**tcct**" to "**tcct**." Each little dance is a uniquely theatrical self, meeting the moment. Exit individually.

Chas: Perform only one "**tcct**" before a unique series of highly theatrical transformations, the duration of which is original, unique, and quintessentially contained.

Ca, Fi, Fra: (Offstage, turn away from the stage.)

Chas: Produce an incantation, not a plea, to draw **Cathy**, **Fiona**, and **Frank** back to stage.

Ca, Fi, Fra: Appear at the edge of the stage. The head is the primary body part that bends, cocks, rolls, twists, and turns.

Chas: Exit incanting.

Fra, Fi, Ca: Travel, in random order. Lift one knee hip-high in front of the body, then the other. Arms are outstretched.

Fra, Ca, or **Fra, Fi,** or **Fi, Ca:** Individually, in one swoop, bend forward, knees bent, say **"fffft."** Simultaneously, stack one hand and then the other hand about two feet from and facing the floor. Arms and body rise incrementally, as a unit, with and sometimes without saying **"fffft."**

Fi, or **Ca,** or **Fra:** Exit performing knee lifts.

Fra, Ca, or **Fra, Fi,** or **Fi, Ca** (continued): Hands are almost overhead before pressing back down to the floor. Follow, original and unique, rolling over a few times, like imagined stop-frame photography.

Fi, or **Ca,** or **Fra,** plus **Chas:** Return to stage rolling like imagined stop-frame photography.

Fra, Fi, Chas, Ca: Reverse rolling direction to spiral up into an airplane stance; arms spread to the sides, one leg bent in front of the body and the other extended behind. Banking is possible.

Fra, Fi, Chas, Ca: In a subdued throaty voice, speak and simultaneously retract unintelligible remarks. Intersperse these remarks with silence and an occasional single quiet note, combining a high and low tone.

*Note: **The Match** hypothesizes the possible with the impossible.*

Fra, Fi, Chas: Individually shift from the airplane into a single gesture made in relation to the others. Sustain voices.

Ca: Remain in the airplane.

Fra, Fi, Chas, Ca: Stand tall, by making incremental adjustments performed in ordinary time. Sound continues.

Fra, Fi, Chas, Ca: Eyes shut.

ACT III

Fra, Fi, Chas, Ca: Eyes open. Ridiculously, combine voice, movement, locomotion, and attitude to spontaneously enact a spunky child's toy, i.e., a jack-in-the-box, a theme and variation combining humor, joy, corn, idiocy, and even embarrassment. Repeat again and again – a challenge to self-esteem.

Fra, Chas, Ca: Exit as toy.

Fi: Continue until toy breaks down, or explodes, or deconstructs, or loses steam, or malfunctions, or transforms, or stops, whatever.

ACT IV

Fra, Ca, Chas: Crawl into view, thus determining the conclusion of **Fiona's** solo.

Note: This is a challenging choice, not a solicitous one.

Fi: Exit and reappear instantly, crawling.

Fi, Ca, Chas, Fra: Crawl anywhere and/or stop, and/or sit, leaning into a hip.

Fra: Stand up and perform, matching nothing with everything.

Ca, Chas, Fi: Do not look at **Frank**.

Fra: Just for a moment, salute the audience.

The lights go out.

June 2006

The following text is a portrait of the dancer Catherine Legrand. It was a journal entry made during my vacation in Bretagne with Catherine and her family.

There are two front doors to the house. Through one is an alcove for shoes and coats. Once past the entryway, everyone is barefoot. I am the only one with socks, sometimes two pairs, and thank god for the Morland sheepskin slippers from Glastonbury that I bought in Brussels last November.

Through the other door is the kitchen. There is a small table for four, around which we have eaten many meals: breakfast, lunch, snack, and dinner. Each meal is served with a tablecloth and cloth napkins, and an assortment of platters, dessert-sized plates, and bowls. Catherine's collection is large and visible on shelves like bookcases, opposite the front door. There are unmatched teacups on hooks and one long row of tall teapots and small, medium, and large bowls precariously stacked. I haven't broken a dish, a testament to my awe. Catherine has had an obviously long and loving relationship with her kitchenware. I know she has given a lot of thought to each dish because I watched her shopping one Sunday morning at an open market in Angers, France.

In an area around the sink and stove are small square floor tiles. They are a magnificent combination of colors: salmon, brown, butter yellow, mustard, burnt orange, and bird's egg blue. When I complimented Catherine on the tile palette, she proudly responded, "I peeked the kollors." On nearby beaches are tiny snail shells of the same colors as the floor tiles. Catherine claims it is a coincidence. The rest of the floor throughout the house is wood.

I ate my first real crepe, hot off the kitchen griddle, with sugar and lemon, its surface texture that of the head of a penis. Of course, I did not say that to Catherine, who stood at the stove in an apron, spooning the smooth batter from its bowl to the griddle, watching it turn to the texture of tissue paper before lifting and turning it to cook on the other side before lifting it again and gently passing it to a plate to spread it with sugar, squeezing lemon over the sugar, and softly wrapping it like a papoose. Which brings me to my vacation in Bretagne.

Catherine and I arrived from Angers after two weeks of coaching seven solo adaptations of "O, O" for seven French dancers who were also learning an adaptation of the group dance "O, O." We would return to Angers in one week in order to continue working with the full cast.

We took the train to Le Mans and then another four-hour train to Morlais. Most of it we spent in the bar, on stools facing the window, which, although uncomfortable, was a great way to see the passing countryside. When we got to Morlais, Catherine picked up her car and we drove for forty more minutes before we reached her house, where her mother stayed with the children until Catherine returned with her guest from Texas, who cannot speak French and puts little effort into listening.

But I wanted to put myself in that situation. I cannot remember the last time I have spent any meaningful amount of time within a family with children. If I am around children, it is always in the context of a brief visit with the parents, who are my friends. Being here, watching and listening to Catherine with her two children, being part of family life, bound by it, having a structure without creating one, having the privilege to live it at any depth I chose is like another universe, not another place. And so I feel a huge amount of gratitude for the opportunity to be brought into the structure of someone else's life as a vacation from mine. It has given me space to reflect on my own history with mothering. As an example, Rose has an ear infection from the tiny blue flowerette earring she has been wearing. I watch as Catherine administers to her pain, having close at hand several antiseptic options to use to allay Rose's fears. And I remember that I never even kept a thermometer in my house as a way to convince myself that Savannah was not sick, and she was, often. I still do not keep a thermometer in my house. It is only recently that I bought Band-Aids! And I rarely thought of going to the pharmacy to ask advice when she was ill, or advice on what over-the-counter drugs to buy, although I remember Robitussin was a cough medicine in frequent use in our household. This is why I veer away from sliding into comparison. I will absolutely kill myself with guilt.

Catherine and her family live in Plounéour-Trez, and they have lived in the house for two years. Soon she and the children will move to Rennes, where her husband moved, so that the family can be closer and traveling made easier, because both parents are performing artists. Getting to Plounéour-Trez felt very much like the stretch between St. Johnsbury and Mad Brook Farm in Vermont.

After hundreds of trips I was always amazed at the extra distance it took to return to the farm.

Plounéour-Trez is in a tiny village. There is a church, a town hall, perhaps a war monument, and a few stores. There are other villages nearby, so it is the combination of them that makes life possible. For instance, the health food store is in one town, the dentist in another, the same for the outdoor market and the children's friends. However, almost every tiny village has a church, and each looks like a variation on a sandcastle. Gray-colored dribbled steeples, where sometimes in the sunlight a yellow-green lichen can be seen distinguishing the contours of the bubbly edifices.

Back to now, for a moment; the sun is getting closer to the horizon, the temperature is dropping, and almost every window and door to the house is open. Catherine just passed my bedroom doors, which also serve as windows, carrying a large aluminum ladder that she had to bring out earlier in order to retrieve a soccer ball that was thrown on the roof by Rose. My fingers and nose are very cold. Every day I have to start bundling up in clothing around this time. At night I need a hot bath before going to bed, otherwise I lie awake plain cold, nothing more. I remembered the hot bath solution after the first night here. I learned it in London, and at Findhorn, in Scotland, and in Denmark, Helsinki, and New York.

I don't want to omit a description of Catherine's mother, Marie Therese. A statuesque figure, gray hair braided down her back, no make-up; a broad-shouldered being, blue eyes and an open expression of strength molded by gentleness. This was the woman who met us at the door when we arrived from Angers. The children, of course, scampered right up and into Catherine's arms, so it was all very busy and forthright. Handing over the children, grandmother to mother, work done, and Marie Therese was off, in her own car, going home, to a house in this same town, which she moved to soon after Catherine settled here.

One day this week we visited her at her house, walking along the shore and then following a field of cauliflower that was ready for harvest. Her garden had flowers and fruit trees and a playscape for the grandchildren. She grew a flower I have never laid eyes on before. It keeps down the mole population. Atop a long fat black stem is a skirt of drooping orange blossoms that look like inverted tulips, at least four or five circling the stem, and on top of them is a crown of green oblong leaves that reach upward. Inside the house were many small oil paintings, and everything else felt FRENCH, COTTAGE, WOMAN, QUIET, HOME.

Now it is time to do the dishes. Something I have loved because I feel that:

1. *I can give Catherine a break from her many, many chores, leaving her more time for her children, and,*
2. *It is a way for me to feel a little warmer because of being around hot water.*

The washing and drying of the dishes is primitive. There is a double sink plus a drain area, yet there is no dish drain. That means that it is possible to wash only a certain number of dishes at a time and think about the interior architecture of the wash tub so that plates can stack, cups can sit inverted, pots don't take up too much room. Thus, it becomes necessary to wash only some dishes at a time and then dry them one by one before washing another load. When removing a dish in order to dry it, it is also important that the rest of the dishes do not collapse.

The kitchen is quite large, and the sink is on the opposite wall from the rows of dishes, plates, and cups. That means, and this is a first, that every dish gets hand dried, one at a time, and walked across the kitchen to its place on the corresponding stack of similar-sized dishes. One at a time, with every cup, saucer, bowl, plate, pot, pot lid, and platter. There are numerous dish towels hanging beside the sink, and they are all soft.

We ate dinner on the porch tonight. I had my scarf wrapped around my head, all zipped up in the same dark clothes I have been wearing for days, nose cold and running. It was only after dinner that Catherine noticed the cold. "Eet tees culd," she said and shrugged her shoulders in her short-sleeved dress before moving us all back into the kitchen.

On Monday we went into town. Catherine had to pick up a train ticket for her trip to Paris, where she will teach a duet she learned in 1993, choreographed by Dominique Bagouet, to two graduating students at the French Academy of Dance. I had to visit her dentist because of a lingering infection around the same molar where I had an infection one year ago when I was in Nottingham. Her dentist, a tall very sweet-looking woman of about forty, also no makeup, moved my molar around with her index finger and said it would have to come out soon. (I still have the molar.) Meanwhile, she wrote a prescription for an antibiotic and mouthwash, which we promptly filled at the pharmacy nearby.

We bought oysters, asking the fisherwoman and a male customer who had just purchased his, if we could and how we could open them. "Surely," they nodded and gave us directions. We bought six large and one dozen small oysters. That night we barely managed to open half of them, this salty, precious food from the sea. The others stayed in a plastic bag and were put on the porch. Tuesday night we had an easier time opening those that were left. That night we ate oysters (the children did not), guacamole, chips, Corbières wine, salad, cheese, and a dessert we bought at a patisserie that we visited so that I could use the toilet. The region is famous for this dessert called Queenaman. The spelling is incorrect, but it is the only way I can remember the name. It is flatish, like a fallen cake weighted down with syrupy brown sugar and butter. Where the almond comes in, I am not sure. I thought, and said aloud even, that I was eating all of my favorite foods at once.

Just as I lay down to sleep, I knew something wasn't right, but I fell asleep nevertheless for a few hours only to awaken so I could try and vomit. All I did was misplace my floating rib so that it stuck wrongly into the muscle around it through the night and for the next day. In the morning, I learned that Catherine also felt sick but not as bad. She ate only two oysters that second night. She went into town, to the pharmacy, and came back with an array of medicines, which we both took, over and over again all day, without eating, plus I had to continue the antibiotic treatment for my gum, and we slept on and off, she upstairs where she sleeps on the other side of a big attic room shared with her children, and me in a spacious room downstairs at the end of the house, near the large bathroom and then the kitchen and then around the corner to the open living-room area with the piano, books, CDs, and children's toys.

In the bathroom Catherine washes clothes in a very small washing machine every day and several times on the days when the sun is shining because there is no dryer, and all the clothes hang on portable clotheslines that get moved around to wherever the sun is shining. This morning she had to place a small boulder at the base of the blue plastic clothesline so that it did not blow over. I have seen the same clothes hanging for days because the weather has mostly been overcast, foggy, and cold.

Today and tomorrow Rose and Joseph are off from school on holiday. There are so many French holidays!

When Catherine is not washing clothes, she is bathing children, hugging and petting them, aside from feeding them endlessly. She runs and plays ball with them, reads to them, and takes them on outings. Today, for instance, we visited Ménéham Beach for the second time. The first time just Catherine and I went, when the children were at school. It is a very special shoreline filled with outcrops of large brown boulders, little islands of them leading into the sea and spotting the coastline. Apparently this was an old fishing village, and there is a small one-room stone house fitted just between two enormous boulders. The water looks clean, and there are lovely-looking beaches and coves with flat walkable smooth sand leading directly into the sea itself. On today's outing a friend of Rose's joined us. She looked to me as I imagine she will look thirty years from now, and I had the thought that most children fall into one of two groupings: those that you know will change in ways you cannot imagine and those that look as they will look forever.

We climbed about, rested, and had relay races, then we took the friend home to the family farm, an experience I will not forget. I thought I would just wait in the car until Catherine found the parents, but then I saw everyone, including the father, bare-chested and bare-footed, in khaki pants, looking like a young boy just off the couch, heading out to the doghouse . . . is what I thought. Why not look at the dog? So I got out of the car and headed into a kennel for hunting dogs, beautiful sweet dogs in clean cages, begging to be petted. The last kennel had five one-week-old pups and the mother. Father said their eyes had just opened.

Then we looked in at a gorgeously attended rabbit house, each little cubicle with a rabbit and a newly chewed cauliflower leaf, with a perfectly stacked wall of single leaves ready to chow down. There was a hen house, dove quarters, a field with a small family of lambs, some peacocks, a gorgeous rooster. The thing about it all was how well cared for everything was and how well tended everything appeared. There was even a pond where the family is raising fish and attracting wild ducks. The house looked out over other pastures and even a town with one of those sandcastle steeples. I was envious, a little. I tried telling Catherine about it and couldn't. It was as if I was seeing a dream of what I want, or once wanted, I am not sure which is true. But it does pull on me in some way. Tonight I learned from Catherine that the mother works in a cheese factory, overseeing the running of its machinery.

I have walked and we have walked a lot. Local excursions, meaning not climbing into a car before the walk, and those walks with Catherine, or Catherine, Rose, and Joseph, to different beaches, with differently configured coastlines. Some trash collects along the shoreline, not much here, but enough to think that it is such a terrible but accurate way to identify where man has been. Today I looked for several hours at a book of Edward Sheriff Curtis's photos of the American Indian. Did they create trash? The first photo in the book was a portrait of a young warrior with what looked like a small scarf at the top of his forehead, tied in a knot. That is the first graphic image to inspire a costume for **Room,** *my solo adaptation of* "O, O."

Catherine screams at the temperature of the sea on her feet. Here I am, in her house, wrapped up in blankets and clothes twenty-four hours a day, and I don't scream when my feet step into the sea. How can this be explained?

One place I have walked nearby includes an empty campground on a hill above the beach. It is a topiary of rectangular-shaped rooms for a camping family's privacy. The hedges are about eight feet tall and half as thick, with only one wall open to a lane leading out of the campground or to the showers and toilets, which were locked. I peed in two different campsites on two different walks. Without people it is like a maze, bringing up images from The Shining. *A terrible place for the imagination and yet inviting to pass through on the way to other beaches farther along.*

I have taken my evening bath. Tonight it was at 10 p.m. The sun sets very late here. There was a tube of green clay in the bathroom, so I spread it on my face, thinking I was alone for the night, only Catherine came downstairs after putting the children to sleep. We exchanged other cream and lotion information.

About Catherine the Great. I first was introduced to Catherine last June, when we performed **The Match**, *plus the solo adaptations, and I performed* **A Lecture on the Performance of Beauty** *at the Montpellier Festival of Dance. I was walking down the street and one of the three dancers from a workshop I taught was walking with her husband and Catherine. The dancer, a close friend of Catherine's, introduced me, telling me that Catherine would be one of the dancers working on* **"O, O."** *I was flooded with excitement because* *of what I knew immediately would be a learning process for me.*

Catherine's countenance is as grand as the sense of feminine mystique that surrounds her. As a performer she leaves room to invent one's own poetry. There is not a trace of anything frivolous about this woman. I watched her solo adaptation of **Room** *just one time in Angers, because she was not ready (she said) to share it with the others. I could not believe how still her adaptation was. My memory has her in one spot on the floor the whole time, and I know for certain that this did not happen. Her stillness was charged with change, shadow, nuance. Shift is too strong a verb. Her performance was closer to theater than dance. It was a breathtaking forty minutes to watch an adaptation of* **Room** *unimagined by me. It was on the same level as Ros Warby's adaptations of my work, only, where Ros can be distinguished by her movements, Catherine can be distinguished by her stillnesses. What a program the two of them would make!*

Plus, she can prepare nori rolls as well as crepes, apple tarte, and guacamole.

Then there are Catherine's outfits, which look as casually considered as slipping on a pair of pajamas. Maybe they are not, of course. But, for instance, one morning she appeared in the kitchen in a mousey brown ankle-length empire-cut tunic; two simple darts for the bodice, a rounded neck. A more uninspired garment does not exist. The tunic brought to mind a remote nunnery in the Alps for French girls aspiring to good deeds and excellent behavior. And throughout the day I could only glimpse at how this frock took on not one single crease or stain but stayed as untouched as it appeared to me, on Catherine, that morning. Then there are combinations, like the knee-length rayon dress with socks and oxfords, or the use of sweatpants worn under the dress. And she likes to wear gloves. She has a red-orange crocheted pair that heightens the effect of any outfit, even during our walks on the beach.

Cleaning up after two children and a houseguest is continuously and invisibly happening. There are never any ignored leftovers. It was only after Catherine the Great served me a limp salad last night, leftover from lunch, that I thought she had gone too far. As a matter of fact, this morning, I proposed that one of the reasons she might identify strongly with my work is because of a shared ethic of resourcefulness. Nothing is wasted in her kitchen, just as nothing of one's practice of attention is wasted in the performance of my dances.

December 2006

My body is capable of so much more than what it can do. For example, the range of sound coming from the piano was more or less constant until John Cage created the prepared piano by introducing different objects that were placed between or on the strings, hammers or dampers. These outside components altered the piano's harmonics and added a whole new gestalt of sound to the world of music. In a similar way the dancer who performs my work has a prepared body, although I am not referring to movement training, physical strength or prowess. A question, crafted by me, is introduced to a dancer who then directs that linear experience into the non-linear assemblage of her/his cellular body. The attractiveness of the question redirects the dancer's attention away from her/his inherently choreographed body, making room for a different mode of performance behavior to arise. The visibility of this altered behavior is experienced in direct proportion to the dancer's willingness, practice, and experience in investing the body with an intelligence that makes use of the question by constantly returning to it. The prepared body is necessary to my choreography and the performance of that choreography, even before my dances are made.

July 2007

What if every cell in your body at once has the potential to choose to surrender the pattern of facing a single direction?

April 2008

What if the question, "What if where I am is what I need?", is not about what you need, but noticing the feedback from the question "what if where I am is what I need?" What if the depth of this question is on the surface?

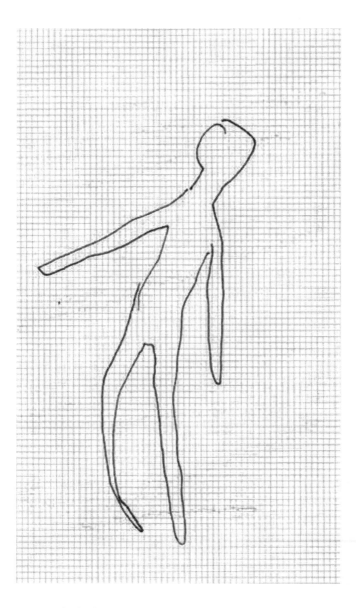

Figure 4 body drawing 1.

April 2008

If I Sing to You

premiere April 3–6, 2008, Dresden, Germany

If I Sing to You was commissioned by The Forsythe Company and co-produced by the Deborah Hay Dance Company, Zodiak Center for New Dance, Helsinki, Howard Gilman Foundation, NY, Maggie Allesee Center for Choreography, FL, with additional support from the Baryshnikov Dance Foundation.

In 2008 *If I Sing to You* was conceived to celebrate ten years of the Solo Performance Commissioning Project (SPCP), which began in 1998 on Whidbey Island, WA.

> *Each year I would choreograph a new solo for up to twenty performers. During a ten-day period in a fairly remote setting, I guided and coached them in the performance of the solo. At the conclusion of the residency each participant signed a contract agreeing to a daily practice of the solo for a minimum of three months prior to his/her first public performance. What was unique about the project was that each dancer had to raise the commissioning fee from within his/ her community. This became part of the selection process by which a performer attended the SPCP. Community, whether family, friends, local, state, or national granting agencies, corporations, became the patrons. All patrons received program acknowledgment every time that year's solo was performed by any of the participating dancers.*

But I was off by a year. I had miscalculated the decade anniversary because in 2003, due to low enrollment, there was no SPCP. While I was trying to figure out if it would ever happen again, I met Gill Clarke, who was co-director of Independent Dance,[1] based in London, and she pressed for the SPCP to resume in Europe in 2004. She had no doubt of its survival there and, through her connection with the Findhorn Community Foundation, it found a new home. All this is to say that **If I Sing to You** *was conceived under a mistaken premise.*

I wanted to choose seven dancers from the many former participants in the SPCP but could not identify seven from this group. None of the male dancers I asked could commit to the six weeks of practice leading to the Dresden premiere of **If I Sing to You**.

The cast[2]

Michelle Boulé

I saw Michelle perform at The Kitchen in 2004 in *dAM-NATION road*, choreographed by Miguel Gutierrez. Struck by the tension between her slippery innocence and managed passion, and without previous knowledge of her as a performer, I invited her to join the cast for *If I Sing to You*, but asked if she would first participate in the 2007

---

[1] Independent Dance (ID) is an artist-led organization providing a responsive framework to support, sustain and stimulate dance artists in their ongoing development as professionals.

[2] In a few later performances Alana Elmer, Chrysa Parkinson, and Ros Warby replaced original cast members who were not free to tour due to other commitments.

SPCP so that she could learn how I work. Members of the Deborah Hay Dance Company Board of Directors, based in Austin, TX, offered to cover her commissioning fee, travel, and accommodations. This was the one and only time such a negotiation happened between the DHDC Board and another individual participating in the SPCP.

Jeanine Durning

I first worked with Jeanine in my 2006 evening length work *"O, O,"* commissioned by Danspace Project for five New York City based dancer/choreographers.[3] Her work ethic was uncompromising and she responded to my material with immediacy and risk, in addition to a fierce and excited intelligence that vivified her body. She seemed able to plunge into and expose her psyche at the same time.

Catherine Legrand

I met Catherine when I was stopped on the street and introduced to her by a mutual friend in Montpellier, France, in 2004, when *The Match* had its European premiere at the Festival Montpellier Danse. Despite the brevity of our encounter, I thought she was the most beautiful woman

---

[3] After *If I Sing to You* Jeanine learned and performed the solo *No Time to Fly*, which prepared her for the trio, *As Holy Sites Go*, performed in Frankfurt, in 2011. She then went on to perform in *As Holy Sites Go/duet*, with Ros Warby, presented in 2011 by Danspace Project in NYC and the Walker Art Center in Minneapolis, MN. She assisted me in teaching *Breaking the Chord* for thirty-four students at the School for New Dance Development in Amsterdam in 2009, and she played a vital role in the Deborah Hay Dance Company's Motion Bank Project in Frankfurt and elsewhere in Europe in 2010–11.

I had ever met. In 2006 I found her again in a dance studio in Angers, France, where Emmanuelle Huynh, then director of Centre National de Danse Contemporaine (CNDC) had assembled a cast of seven French dancer/choreographers to learn a French adaptation of *"O, O."* During this gestation period I came to admire the depth of Catherine's steely calm and an intense inner mystery that clothed her performance of my work.

Juliette Mapp

Like Jeanine, Juliette first worked with me in the New York version of *"O, O"* in 2006. The characteristics of generosity, courage, and beauty filled the space around her dancing and immediately drew me to her. She was rigorous in how she applied her attention to the moment, an attribute that played itself out in stunning stillnesses as well as startling physicality.[4]

Vera Nevanlinna

Vera attended a workshop I taught in 2005 in Vrå, Denmark. She then participated in the 2006 SPCP. She had the most strikingly bizarre comprehension of my work, highlighted by an electricity that seemed to fire uninterruptedly on stage. I think it was her extremely Finnish nature that drove her to uncensored possibility.[5]

---

[4] After *If I Sing to You* Juliette learned and performed the solo *No Time to Fly*, preparing her for the trio, *As Holy Sites Go*, performed in Frankfurt, in 2011.

[5] Two years following *If I Sing to You*, Vera and five other Finnish dancers performed *Lightening*, which was commissioned by Helsinki's Zodiak Center for New Dance and presented in the 2010 Helsinki Festival.

Amelia Reeber

Amelia learned the solos *Music* in the 2001 SPCP and *o beautiful* in the 2002 SPCP. In 2007 I invited her to perform in *Mountain*, an evening-length work for three Seattle-based dancer/choreographers. She was, simply put, a knockout performer, and subtle, funny, sly, regal, carefree, impetuous, testy, and generally absent of any visible ego when she danced.

During the first four weeks of teaching and coaching the dancers in their practice of **If I Sing to You***, I was also editing and making changes to the dance as it developed each day. This took place in February/ March 2008, in Mikhail Baryshnikov's dance studio at the White Oak Plantation in Florida, followed by a second residency at Maggie Allesee National Center for Choreography in Tallahassee, FL. During these four weeks, we would sometimes gather as a group immediately following a practice of the work, and listen as each dancer described her experience within a singular component of choreography. By the conclusion of the Florida residencies I had filled a notebook recording their responses to the entire dance.*

Within the score for **If I Sing to You***, the dancers' feedback appears as Dancer's notes. The combined input from the six dancers is mixed together so that the reader can follow the many different responses to the same moment or movement direction within the choreography. The written feedback reflects the shorthand I needed to apply in order to keep up with their thoughts.*

Because the dance underwent so many big and small changes from when we began and even up to the final performances in New York at the Baryshnikov Arts Center, I edited how the dancers referred to parts of the dance that were no longer relevant. For example, early on there was a movement called, "diving into the waa waa." After awhile it became "without moving slowly five dancers separately dive forward tossed here and there as if in freefall." I changed their early references into this final description although at the moment I wish I had kept "diving into the waa waa."

Make-up and costumes

The full cast was involved in choosing one another's male and female costumes, with input from my project assistant, Laurent Pichaud. For every performance the women had the option to appear wearing their male or female costume. Their choice was made without prior consultation with either the choreographer or other cast members. It was in the dressing room that they learned who was who. The one rule in costuming was that more than one gender be represented on stage. The intention was to layer the dynamics of the choreography through an illusion of momentary contexts and compositional choices, yet I instructed the dancers not to alter anything about their behavior or dancing when performing as men, or boys in some cases. I asked Diane Torr, particularly known as a male impersonator, for help finding someone to teach the cast how to apply male make-up. She suggested Moritz G, a Berlin-based transgender performer.

Working individually with each dancer over several days, Moritz guided them in how to apply male facial hair, from eyebrows and sideburns to five o'clock shadow.

Running time

1 hour to 1 hour 20 minutes without intermission. The duration of the performance depended on the size of the stage and the presence of both the audience and the dancers. Eighty percent of the solos and duets were spontaneously cast during each performance, meaning that any dancer(s) had the power to step up to perform a solo or duet the moment that solo or duet unfolded in the choreography.[6] This meant that it was not possible for the lighting/sound technician to take cues from a particular dancer, a predetermined time, or where the dancers were onstage. Cues were mainly determined by subtle or sudden movement changes.

Songs

Several months prior to teaching the dance, each performer was asked to sing a song every day, for twenty seconds or less, beginning with the words "If I Sing to You," until one song stood out as THE song. The dancer's criteria for choosing THE song was the insight gained each time she repeated it. On our first day together in the studio in Florida, I selected three of the six songs to include in the choreography.

---

[6] Eleven of the spontaneously cast solos/duets were narrowed to nine after repeated performances of *If I Sing to You*.

Sound

Five recordings, using only the dancers' voices, were played at prescribed intervals in the choreography. They are listed in the order they were heard:

1. intermittent gibberish spoken like a short prayer;
2. individually produced spontaneous songs;
3. singing a collectively composed fake hymn together;
4. vocal reproductions of the dancers' feet lightly tapping the floor, which ended up sounding like the woods in summer;
5. Amelia singing her song alone.

The volume level was barely audible, so that audiences were not sure whether or not they were hearing sound from outside the theater, in their minds, or from elsewhere in the audience. The speakers were not visible. One was behind the stage, out of sight, facing the audience. Another was above the stage, facing down onto it. There were speakers offstage right and left, facing the stage. One or more were behind the audience, either facing or not facing the stage, depending on how the sound carried in the theater. A change in font indicates the start and stop of each recording in the written score.

The dance

Entering the theater from the lobby, the audience sees the dancers onstage, their backs turned to them. They stand like ordinary people, more or less shoulder to shoulder, positioned in a shallow curve near the front of the stage but not at its center. Their barely discernable voices intermittently produce brief unintelligible phrases, spoken like a short prayer. Played at minimal volume, a pre-recording of these similarly produced sounds comes from two upstage speakers while the cast faces upstage. The recordings are then transferred to two speakers behind the audience as the dancers turn to face downstage. Based on when a theater is willing to open its doors prior to a performance, this opening can be as long as ten minutes. For the dancers it is their opportunity to practice juggling a handful of questions, or internal directives, that guide them through their performance. Their fundamental prop is "What if every cell in my body at once has the potential to dialogue with everything I see and cannot see?" By the time the audience is seated, the dancers have turned toward them.

The challenge is how to remain alert and interested in being onstage for an extended period of time with so little to do. "What if every cell in my body at once has the potential to dialogue with everything I see and cannot see?" The cast is experienced in the futility of looking for answers to the question and wary of finding themselves trapped by thinking they know what they are doing. They therefore attend to a self-generated energy that rises from the ineffability of the question in the reconfigured cellular body.

I was once at a dinner party in southern California where eight women sat comfortably around a table. Two women were in a dialogue that drew the attention of the rest of us. I have no memory of the subject matter but have a vivid recollection of being frozen by the thought that I had never experienced a true dialogue before, either hearing one or being a participant. It was as if I was listening to a game of chess, without its ruthless competitiveness. There was room for thought, provocation, and insight. Neither woman seemed anxious to prove anything nor was there evidence of anger or hostility. And I clearly remember a third entirely unforeseen component being birthed through their shared input.

At the time in the studio I was working with the concept of prayer and its relevance in my life. I had difficulty using the word "prayer," let alone accessing prayer as a verb. But when I substituted the word "dialogue" for "prayer" my resistance subsided. The word "dialogue" is earthy, civilized, dynamic, non-hierarchical, and more than one-sided. Alone in the studio, my cellular experience of dialogue was neither directional nor translatable. What if every cell in my body at once has the potential to dialogue with everything I see and cannot see? In other words, I am not looking at the world, I am participating in it.

Other movement directions as the dancers turn to face the audience? A sparsely administered non-consequential leg or arm movement slips in and out of view, with a limit of three movements per performer. In addition, Juliette laughs two separate times. Jeanine lies on her side. She may dialogue from there before standing again. And finally, Catherine, seeing the audience seated, sings her version of "If I Sing to You." The recorded dialogues conclude. Michelle will at times join Catherine singing.

"And, if I sing to you
all the things that I see,
soon you would see, you would see
so many things about you."

Dancers' notes: The opening dialogue has transformed
with the presence of the audience. In the studio we would
begin with silence and dialogue with that silence. Now,
when the doors actually open, sound and energy pour in.
I hear people rushing to their seats. I am aware of their
finding us in practice already onstage. If I speak loud
enough for everyone to hear I would have to shout. The
audience begins to hear us as they grow quiet. Sometimes
they laugh. Sometimes they are looking so intently. I
think it has to do with our costuming. Imagining people entering the theater yet having my back to the audience helps shift my sense of time. It disappears. I am not
waiting. It is helpful to dialogue with what I cannot see
because then there is less anticipation of things that happen. I am conscious of how my sounds shake the space
as I allow them to come as they come. We are trees or
drops of water falling into other water. I like how we
stand so closely now. In the group I hear the first person
talking and then there is laughing which keeps opening
my hearing and makes me freer with my whole body.
The movements feel light. I am turning to face front and
I do not have to think about it. I am balancing the challenge of using the questions as a lens, with the concrete-
ness of everything I see. Not getting trapped or lost in the
sound of my own voice and how my mouth just behaves
correctly. It is getting easier in that the dialogue can be

whatever, not prayer. My body is relaxed. No decisions. I love seeing others. Inviting being seen. We stand here. You watch us. We watch you. It is so funny to me. I love to see the audience, to have the lights on. My song comes when it comes. My question is how not to end at the end of the song.

After Juliette laughs twice, and Jeanine gets up, and Catherine sings her song, the dancers simultaneously look up to see an imagined phantom dance dropping from above before splitting into six parts, spatially separating the cast, one dancer per part. The repetition of an indistinct upbeat note, particular to each dancer, represents the moment each dancer's separate apparition alights here and there while bouncing around the stage. Following its imagined whereabouts each of the six dancers arrives upstage, away from the audience, and with rigorous and consistent work, and many details to pack in, she wrestles, envelops, and grounds her partial dance, incorporating it into her, from its conclusion through to its beginning by reversing her movement momentum and phrasing.

My directions are devices for stimulating a kind of activity onstage. The dancers are aware of my narrative traps and they work to stay clear of being swallowed by them. In other words, recognizable movement is not an element in my work. My choice is to create an atmosphere that maintains a flow of indefinable logic for the dancers and audiences alike.

No hesitation, no reconsideration comes as the number of questions juggled by the dancer has increased over the years. My first impulse, still, is to align all the questions before following the choreographed directions. What results is a movement pattern based on how I think the questions shape what I think the choreography should look like. No hesitation, no reconsideration forces me to notice how I can learn from my body. This directive is a fabulous tool for practicing the performance of the same material over time.

Dancers' notes: My dialogue with all there is gets carried into the space with the phantom dance part. The whole experience turns more collective in its sudden momentum. I can get lost when the phantom dance enters. Am I here or there? I am aware of changes in space with the apparition's appearance. I feel pulled, slightly schizophrenic. A global practice of dialogue reduces to a singularity of attention to our phantom part. Vaudevillian, sound to match action, which I like. The sounds we are making open up my perspective of space in a different way. The information coming at me is as if it is pixelated, like having to process more and more quickly. Conflict actually. I know I have to go somewhere and I want to go somewhere else. My body is just a consequence of this activity. It is a very light sensation. I don't know what is happening in my body.

Except for a soloist who continues to wring her portion of the phantom dance from thin air, the other five dancers circle the periphery of the stage, running counterclockwise, as if holding the shell of their weightless captured apparition.

At some point after we began touring I asked Juliette to be the lone soloist left to wrestle and wring from nowhere her phantom part. My intervention was based on two observations.

1) *The dance would often drag soon after all six performers were wrestling their appropriated phantom. It stopped being interesting very quickly. One dancer was to step up to the solo that would keep the struggle going as the rest of the cast stopped wrestling and circled the stage. No one could recognize who had begun the solo because everyone was wrestling. By default it was the dancer who could hold out the longest, thwacking away in space, who became the soloist. Assigning this solo to Juliette freed the cast and the dance from the pall of uncertainty in the choreographed sequence of events.*

2) *Juliette reduced me to tears laughing whenever she tackled the partial phantom. She was not about to lose her share of the booty. Swinging, flailing, and kicking, especially when dressed in her black leather jacket that slid right and left off her shoulders with her white shirt and red tie loosening; her moustache and heavy brows made her stand out firmly as a figure not to be messed with.*

They spread non-uniformly downstage, facing the audience, and are soon joined by the soloist. Lifted up from below, or lowered down from above, a whole intact invisible dance is drawn into each woman's welcoming body. Ancient voices whisper intermittent bits of support and wisdom: "sdlfjoetm klm; kh," from within their six singular embodiments.

> *The dancer navigates between the sobriety required to maintain the impossibility of doing a movement "right" and the thrill from not being asked to.*

Dancers' notes: I am excited about not knowing where I will end up in the line. We are putting the dance into our bodies and into space. I enjoy it and wish I could go all the way to my toes and all the way up with the inhabitation. I am working on getting the dance into my whole body because my arms get tired. I am sometimes confused by the seriousness and humor of it. It seems that this is often the case in the dance. Listening to time and space feels good. I feel torn trying to balance all parts. The ancient voice gives me tension. I hear it and try to be calm. My ancient voice feels far away. It takes a while to find a voice. When everyone arrives downstage it is a powerful feeling which helps me find my voice. Our ancient voices become a song. It is like an image from a film. I hear our music. Everyone is a different creature. My voice gives my nervous system attention. Time to think about dance differently. I may be habitual with the voice I use but I know it can be anything. My ancient voice feels familiar, wise, telling me I do not know what, but advice. I feel comfortable in that.

With profoundly delicate care, each dancer transports her incarnated dance along one of six single curved paths from downstage to up.

"What if every cell in my body at once has the potential to choose to surrender the pattern, and it is just a pattern, of locating myself in relation to a single direction?" The solo **Room**, *2005, performed in the round, was conceived to help me undo the performance behavior where I identified front as if it was a fixed condition that had greater value than elsewhere onstage. The same was true when I was alone in a studio. As a result, when not facing front, the importance of my visual field diminished without my even realizing it.*

Dancers' notes: There is a lot to carry and I enjoy the fullness of it. I have to remember to invite being seen carrying the dance. My body feels arbitrary. Do I even need to move? I love the carrying. It is necessary to me. I feel proud and nurturing. I feel like the imaginary inhabitation and curve is a way of lining up the questions in ways other than dialogue. It supports the inclusivity of space and audience. The moment of going into the curve is like a spatial warp – space opens. I like to see everyone working on the curve and the intersections between us. Lots of tension seeing others, not tense, but charged. The sense of 360-degree awareness becomes strong in the curved path. Being in this dance is different. I often do not know what happens next. It is remarkable to me. I feel grateful for that. The questions make that happen. I liked seeing space as what distinguishes the curve. I think beautiful, the whole dance in my body. I love my curve. Sometimes I depend on it. It is easy. Sometimes I am in a duet. I am enjoying the multiple curves in the space and how my body reflects the other curves. Curve begins as an unknown and yet I can depend on it. I want to make it longer. I want to know where it is and to make that clear. It is the first moment I feel the whole space.

Poetry unfolds along six separately revealed zigzag paths that provide a downstage passage for each dancer. Just as every word in a poem appears in relation to every other word, every movement is performed in relation to every other movement. The dancer tries not to predetermine the zigzag, the movement, or attach to a meaning. Like poetry, there is time for the audience to contemplate the many possible associations within any moment and to notice innuendo and phrasing.

Dancers' notes: The fluidity from curve into poetry feels satisfying. No space between one thing ending and another beginning. If I am upstage and the only one there, then all I have to do is see poetry in the others and mine begins naturally. It modulates in a really nice way. At first the differences were so big but as we work more I see more, like the collectivity of the poem and seeing every movement as relevant. It is also so in the world. Stillness in poetry helps me too. The space feels open even when we are grouped tightly. Poetry is delicious. Thinking of it not in terms of words in poems but the space between the words, and the punctuation within a poem. I love listening in this way. We are a band. Not a garage band. I was in one once and played drums. We are an orchestra or a really good band. Today it is poetry I don't relate to but I am glad that it exists. Like bad poetry, I am still glad it exists. I enjoy poetry but feel the limitation of the stage. Something about poetry unfolding closer and closer to the audience makes me want to keep it going. I can see everybody and it is very helpful to think about the word poetry and nothing more. I have this sensation of how simple and pleasurable this is for everybody.

In more or less a line facing the audience, the performers simultaneously turn away and briefly revisit their hushed unintelligible dialogue with all there is. Abruptly, voices representing their dark side spew forth and then quickly subside.

Dancers' notes: I feel like I have to stop the poetry and start the dialogue sooner. I am caught by the return of the dialogue but not always. We can't get to the dialogue. Our line feels off. To return to the dialogue is like a harmonic convergence. I don't realize I am waiting for it to arrive. And the brevity of it works to arouse the dark side. There is just enough time with the dialogue before it is eclipsed by the dark side. It is almost like the dark side is looking for me and this makes it feel more organic in terms of my voice and body. I like feeling so much. The dark side feels like evil, but also conflict. Like to have the dark side must mean an opposition to something and that feels like a unique moment in the song of the whole dance. How is it that the back of my body can include and mutate into the dark side? I am conscious of my back to the audience. It comes alive when I hear our dialogue. I feel allowed to enter the dark side because my back is turned to the audience.

Two dancers spin out from the line, driving themselves here and there onstage and at its edges, participating in playing out whatever they imagine, think, believe, at that moment, to be their dark side. This is the closest they get to representation in the dance. Their movement behavior is brutal, loud, sexist, vulgar, disdainful, and demeaning. Using fake language they shout, command, and insult. Their silences are particularly foreboding. The four remaining dancers travel in a line across stage, more or less shoulder to shoulder, turning without turning on half-toe, and making sporadically clipped cries. They are like a curtain beyond which the dark side duet is intermittently hidden. Still flaunting their dark side, the duet separates to become one and the other side of a bogus proscenium near center stage. A moment later a former curtain dancer runs upstage behind the fake proscenium in order to enter through and remain within its frame to perform her dark side. The three remaining dancers form a tighter curtain, one beside the other with their backs to the audience. The soles of their shoes brush the floor as they travel across stage and back to its center in order to obscure the soloist within the phony proscenium and eventually still the collected group activity.

As with Juliette earlier in the dance, once we began touring, I intervened and assigned Amelia the dark side solo. My decision was based on two observations.

1) *The two dancers who just ended a vulgar and manic duet that usually succeeded in getting the audiences hyped up are now obscured by four*

curtain dancers teetering on their toes center stage. At this point, one dancer from the quartet was to step up to a solo version of the duet and perform with equal impropriety. Their understandable hesitancy was excruciating for me to witness. The teetering curtain looked like a sinking ship caught in the middle of an ocean.

2) *Whenever Amelia rose to the occasion I laughed till it hurt. A cross between Jerry Lewis and Buster Keaton seemed to bewitch her.*

Dancers' notes: When the duet begins, and we face the two dancers, I feel a lot of mutation in my body. It feels like I am flipped on my back as I mutate into a curtain. To turn, suffer, cry, they are all separate experiences. Where is that in relation to the audience? I am physically aware of whether or not I am obstructing the action onstage. I feel as the curtain that my crying can't be heard. I was surprised watching today because I heard a cry. It made me think of the netherworld, of subterraneous workings. I want to jump into the duet but hold back and either I jump in or I deflate into curtain. Sometimes in the dark side I think I stop myself from going over the top. As the tight curtain, once the solo starts, I feel like a janitor coming in and sweeping up the place. Feels nonchalant. As the soloist I do not want to be covered by the curtain. I am confused about the proscenium. Does the soloist influence the proscenium? I want independence as the proscenium. The dark side gives me energy and clarity. It grounds me in a different way and the whole piece changes. I eat your eyeballs and fingers. A witch puts children in an enclosed area. The witch is blind. The children stick pencils through the fence, instead of their fingers, so the witch thinks they have not put on weight. I am not playing with silence enough. Maybe because of what you said about our voices bringing us into our bodies. I don't know how I will be in my body without the sound of the dark side. As the proscenium I primarily think of a curtain, holding the space and trying to remain with the dark side. It is helpful to keep my dark side voice going, mostly to keep myself mutating. As an old heavy velvet curtain I become aware of the soloist and begin to mutate with her rather than maintaining the curtain. I feel supported and inspired by the quiet side of the dark side. As curtain, I have the feeling of quiet coming. A calm is set and this is the beginning of waiting but not waiting. I thought I would die from anticipation. Then all that work we did on not anticipating changed things for me. I am practicing emptying and being ready.

A shorter than short single note is produced in chorus by the dancers. It punctuates the stillness and sends the dancers into string-on-fire, the term used to inspire the movement, although, looking at the dancers, you would not find yourself thinking they look like strings on fire. The language describes the passion and speed of their jig-like dancing; upright, arms at their sides, they primarily use their feet, arhythmically. Moving in two flanks, the former curtain trio travels upstage while the dark side soloist and former fake proscenium duet travel as a trio downstage. Everyone is making an elongated and narrow U-shaped path along which continually engaged, fast-paced, irregularly timed movement of the feet prevails. Attention to the slight curve at the end of the first leg of the U is collectively achieved. Completing the U, two synchronized steps lead into a second U-shaped path. This time, the former dark side soloist travels upstage, making a quartet of the former curtain. Before the final leg of the second U is completed, all paths diverge sharply and spread across the stage.

> *Describing movement as it unfolds in my dances, as I do in this score, only brushes the surface of what happens onstage. It is what I cannot name or point at in watching how a dancer performs that keeps me interested in dance. My choreography is embedded with invisible directives that invite the performer to constantly be in the act of reorganizing herself. The directives are tools that stimulate a meaningful engagement between the dancer and all there is.*

Dancers' notes: I am glad the single note is over because it is always a glancing disappointment before the string-on-fire. Is our single sound good enough? Shall I go or not? Usually I know but sometimes there is a hesitation that feels bad. Fascinating to work on and amazingly hard. I am waiting, which is different from when we are practicing the sound separate from the run of the piece. I feel so unstable. Am I one person or the group? I listen to people swallowing and breathing, letting it go, letting it be taken care of, something larger than my attention to the task. The short note is a part of the music of whole dance. When the moment is right the note happens and either I produce it and everyone follows, or not, or we all sound the note together. This keeps me connected to the piece rather than just this moment. It helps to read the others practicing what I am practicing. There is a moment after our single note where I am so happy it is over that I tend to drop into my body. At this moment, inviting being seen from the temples has been useful. I enjoy being so convinced that I am a string-on-fire. String-on-fire is a burning strip, almost chasing me, leading to the dynamite. Also surprised by what can happen in my lower limbs and how hard it is to stay in line. It becomes fuzzy when I forget the straight lines. The integrity of the spatial relationship we all share in string-on-fire is very satisfying to me. Here comes the little curve and the memory of waterslides. It is as if our momentum shifts but it really doesn't. It is fun and light. I feel joy in my upper body and love watching others. It feels like we are trying to have an orgasm together. But we will never get it. Serious work. The sound of our shoes on the wood floor changes so much. It becomes musical, like an old swing band. Without thinking of it as music, it just is music.

Jeanine arrives first and the others fill the stage standing at the same angle, as if they are a chorus of eighty without room to face the audience directly. Jeanine sings her version of "If I Sing to You."

If I sing to you
Would you want me to stay with you?
Would you want me to play and do
All the things that we used to do?

When her song ends, Michelle, Amelia, and Catherine join her in singing a collectively composed hymn. Vera and Juliette lip-synch.

By tilting her face upwards, each dancer chooses when to turn the hymn into a spontaneous, repeatable, non-translatable song. Recordings of individual songs mix with the live singers and are audible from one or two speakers hung above the stage. It seems as if the dancers, with upraised heads, are singing with the voices that reach them from above. Partway through the duration of these artless songs, mouths of comedy and tragedy alternate on the dancers' faces. The pre-recorded songs phase out. A singing soloist bursts from the chorus in a flurry of bizarre airborne activity. A male-costumed dancer cannot perform this solo. Powerfully, passionately, in a high-pitched voice, she expresses herself with intermittent calls. Her movement and voice play on phony misplaced American Indian/Bedouin imagery. She rides atop irregularly produced ritual-like steps and hops, her arms and fingers spread and retract interruptedly. Her path, like a tightly curled pubic hair, weaves tightly through space and the other dancers. The solo ends with a three-second voice and body mumble, joined by the ensemble of three-second mumblers.

Figure 5 ***If I Sing to You.*** Left to right: Jeanine Durning,
Catherine Legrand, Michelle Boulé, Amelia Reeber
(© Sylvio Dittrich, 2008).

Dancers' notes: Tricky jumping into the hymn, maybe
because I chose to keep my feet moving in string-on-fire
until I begin singing. A hymn. What is a hymn? Keeping this
word in mind I am open to what it may mean. Sometimes I
feel removed or joking about it. I feel singular in the choral
arrangement and not seeing. My own song sounds folksy,
like a hoedown. I love being able to hear what is coming
out. Changing faces changes the sound of my song. The
soloist racing by me feels great. I make choices to notice
her and let it go. Being affected without having to do anything about it. I like to drop my song for a moment and
then start again. I hear it in this field of songs and wonder
if the audience just hears a field of songs? Now that I lip
sync the hymn, I feel a huge tension lifted. I feel like I am
singing. I enjoy it when I can shift into seeing my personal
song in conjunction with how I am seeing and like that the

song repeats. Hearing the hymn makes the personal song so rich. It feels good to have both comedy and tragedy faces. There is no gap between the hymn and personal song. It reminds me of the ocean and the space around the ocean. It is a challenge to keep the song the same when comedy and tragedy faces occur. I notice I lower my voice in tragedy and raise it in comedy. Sometimes so much attention to what I am hearing that I don't hear my own music. I get images of us in robes and also a backup band. I haven't done the solo in awhile because my energy goes to an extreme. I get surprised by having to maintain the tightly curled path. It seems that that one should fill the whole space. Sometimes it feels schizophrenic but it is all of that that makes it what it is. I like that the calling expands space because it helps me stay connected to others. It should not be alarming. I feel the personal song meeting the calling or that the calling is always there and we are just hearing it now. Sometimes I notice my personal song warps when it meets the calling. The sounds physically hit each other and become something else for awhile.

Music begins. The movement is called music because the dancers collaboratively choose when and how they will produce sound made by their shoes tapping on the stage floor. They collectively step about on half-toe, forming a foursome and a duet before merging into a single ensemble. I could easily recommend that an audience member close his/her eyes during music, in order to hear the dance.

Three variations occur during music, each initiated by a different dancer. As soon as it begins the other cast members spatially frame the soloist like a chorus. When a variation ends the cast returns to music until the next variation emerges.

The formation of a chorus can also isolate and thus determine one of the three variations. The chorus remains true to vocally reproducing the sounds of their feet tapping the stage floor while attentively noting the performance of the variation. The three variations occur in almost any order.

1. A dancer leans forward partway, with her head lowered. Without going anywhere she performs blurry movement in blurry time and blurry space.

Figure 6 ***If I Sing to You.*** Left to right: Amelia Reeber, Jeanine Durning, Juliette Mapp, Vera Nevanlinna, and, in front, Michelle Boulé (© Anna van Kooij, 2008).

2. Two women isolate themselves or are isolated by the group. They move uniformly to the floor, make physical contact there and then rise. During the duet the audience hears the recording of the vocal re-enactment of the dancers tapping feet that sounds a little bit like the woods in summer. At the end of the duet the recording disappears.

3. A single dancer, near the floor, barks ferociously at the audience, the other dancers, and unoccupied space. Her silence is as ferocious as her barking. Her movements do not correspond to the passion behind the bark. The dog cannot be the first variation.

One of three non-repeatable strategies for morphing concludes each variation.

1. The variation morphs towards the chorus.
2. The chorus morphs towards the variation.
3. The variation and the chorus morph toward each other in space.

Don't try to be interesting runs parallel to don't try to be creative. The language is a deliberate jab at the very foundation of modern dance pedagogy that promotes creative movement. What if how I perceive is my creativity at work? This internal directive reflects an aesthetic preference that favors an enlargement of the experience of dancing, for dancer and audience, beyond what the body can achieve through movement. For example, can I perceive how my whole body is in a constant state of reorganization in relation to itself, in space, as time passes, in relation to the other dancers and the audience?

Dancers' notes: After so much time looking up, my seeing and hearing feels vast. It takes a little time to go from looking up to hearing the music of our tapping feet. My feet make music before I register the music. I like to come into the music rather than determining what it is. It feels like a shift downward. I like going into the quartet and duet before merging the two. It is like a sudden finding of architecture. It is always a huge adjustment to go from looking up in the personal song to spreading horizontally in music that I forget the duet and quartet. I love the music here. It is as if I am sitting on a porch relaxing, and listening to the sound of wind effecting life around me. Trying to stay together feels like being on a skateboard. The clarity of this section is satisfying to see. It is challenging and maybe seductive to try and use our voices to represent the sound of our shoes on the floor. I mean really trying to go into what it really sounds like. Sometimes during the dog solo, the barking is so loud I cannot hear us. How do I decide to do the duet? I can't decide. I can't make the opportunity happen but I stay open to what happens. I go down to the floor and someone will go down with me. The duet arrives without a decision. I have never gone into a duet without it working that way. I like the intimacy of the events of the structure now, like a huge magnifying glass over the group. There is such empathy within the variations, the production of our sounds, and in our clear physical relationship within the group. What is appearing on our faces? Can we go on with empathy because in the dog solo my face is reactive. I actually enjoy perceiving the blurry dance as blurry. It feels like not having to do anything and this heightens my understanding of so much in the dance. It feels great to be part of a chorus for the soloist with an audience. Even though I am looking at the solo, my body perceives the whole space.

When the three variations are finished, the music of tapping shoes continues but without sound. As if coming from far away, the recording of the group singing their hymn is just audible throughout the theater. Still tapping without sound, the group makes a counterclockwise sweep of the stage, ending in an uneven line in front of the audience. Five dancers separately dive forward, tossed here and there as if in freefall, with a caveat that they not use their arms. The recording ends. Reaching the floor, still flying, their legs float fuzzily side by side before the

Figure 7 *If I Sing to You.* Left to right: Jeanine Durning, Vera Nevanlinna, Michelle Boulé, and Amelia Reeber (© Anna van Kooij, 2008).

audience while their heads perch without support. The sixth dancer continues performing music, soundlessly, keenly aware of her command of time, and where she pauses and chooses her steps in relation to the dancers, the stage, and the audience.

Dancers' notes: In our sweep of space I hear the music of our footsteps even though it is silent. I am aware that the curve we are making is not so defined. It is a moment when sound resonates in my body. Freefall is fun, like I could get lost in space, but I have to get to the floor. My imagination is expansive and my body is riding and feeling slightly cartoonish. Being on the floor feels so different as a continuation of freefall. There is a hard head wind. My hair is blowing back. Wouldn't it be funny if our clothing and wigs were blown back and off? Not using my arms makes it more of what it is. Maybe I need to attend more to not getting lost.

Regaining momentum, the five dancers individually fly to their feet to join the upright stepping soloist. They perform a plethora of other dances' endings that stubbornly adhere to the experience of all dancers everywhere. A final fake ending pose, unique to each performer, clicks into place simultaneously. Stillness remains in effect for longer than audiences are prone to expect. At its best, there is time for the viewer to see that there is no quantifiable difference between movement and stillness.

> *The same experiment, different experience, is an out-growth of the question, "what if I see you practicing what I am practicing?" It is a crucial self-regulated*

directive within my ensemble work. The same experiment means that each dancer recognizes that she is working with the same question as every other cast member and that the question comes in and out of focus for everyone. At the same time the dancer is aware that her experience of the question is unique to her, just as it is unique for each member of the cast.

Dancers' notes: We have been doing this since the beginning and now it is real fake choreography. A conviction. It feels like a challenge to engage with others during the fake choreography. I have an array of choreographic references. It is easier not to be cute or be funny. This is a place where we have to do something. I like the endeavor. We have this common pool. Why does this happen in the dance? It's a bit character producing. Bad Dance. Stupid. We have this inside info that is not an ending. What helps is to not look for our collective ending. It just comes. I just realized I think of fake choreography as a thing in itself and not part of the whole dance. Today with a guest I find myself thinking about time and stillness. I never think these thoughts without guests present. I become aware of time and how long different sections are in different parts of the dance. It helps to invite being seen.

In a sole uniform move, the dancers face the audience, bringing their arms to their sides. Whoever is furthest stage left performs an inconspicuously dazzling dance in a blurry space, highlighted by and in contrast to the stillness of the group.

One at a time, from stage right to left, Michelle, Catherine, Amelia, Vera, Juliette, and Jeanine form a line holding hands facing the audience. How and where onstage they arrive in this order holding hands is determined by two acts surrounded by many unforeseen options that the choreographer never imagined.

1. From where she is standing, the dancer most down-stage chooses to extend her right, left, or both hands, holding it, or them, out in space. It is also possible for her to walk elsewhere onstage before extending a hand or both hands.

2. Another dancer determines when to walk to and stand beside or take the outreached hand in hers. This dancer, who chooses to read the gesture as specific to her, can instead choose to extend her other hand.

When Juliette and Jeanine take hands, they face one another, whispering between themselves, while everyone else faces the audience.

Dancers' notes: Standing feels like a place of choice. When will it end? Decisions just get made. Momentary relief. Feels like I get to see so much. Feels alive. Not dropped. Simple. Satisfying. Sometimes a geometry is present in the sense of a chess game. I am working so much. It feels like time is not passing. I haven't yet worried about time passing. No anticipation, like in the earlier single note. I feel people passing around me and my body in relation to other bodies in relation to audience. Today was the first time I decided to extend my hand and I wasn't sure where I would go. Today I take Juliette's hand. Usually I calculate where to go and how it will work. I love the formality of standing and with it a great satisfaction in standing with the group. It feels classical. A real sense of pride. Like Serenade will start. Stepping up to inviting being seen helps me a lot. Not in terms of postural but what is revealed. I love to not know what will happen. Taking of hands, enjoying the metaphor of the chess game and the subtle shifting narratives of who goes with who. Looking at Jeanine, I have to surrender everything. All I imagine is this huge event transpiring behind me. Complex and great for me and Jeanine to be looking at each other for so long and so different to have Vera on one side and Jeanine on the other. Seems nice that there are times when we don't know and the audience does not know at the same time. There is balance in taking hands. Today I had a slight fear, that was okay. It always works out. It is playful not heavy. Maybe I become a caretaker. I want everyone to take hands. I hope my senses are correct about when to begin singing. It is a game that does not get boring. It is constantly feeding something. I get feedback that my face is fixed and I am free of that now. Nothing feels like a mistake. It is like a continuum from the fake ending. To step up, to not finish, or mark it any way, a continuum with different rhythms. I am here and at this moment I think I should move to change but generally I do not. Why? Because I think you want us to go further and we are still trying it and maybe this is the moment to push that.

Amelia chooses the moment when all held hands release, causing a semi-shock wave of reactions up and down the line.

Dancers' notes: Today's shock was not a shock. Amelia doesn't get shocked. I let go of my behavior around shock and experienced it more as through a vaseline lens. I get an echo of shock down the line. I want to be shocked and surprised. There is room for me to play here. If I stand in silence for too long or sing for too long I am afraid the section will go on too long. This thing that is shock but then it's not a shock, a myriad of interpretations happen. I think I will break Catherine's fingers. Juliette grabs my hands. Jeanine feels the weight of Juliette's whole body in her hand.

A sensual dance ensues.

> *Depending on whom you ask, of course, performing a sensual dance can be embarrassing, a dream come true, provoking, silly, inhibiting, etc. I have often used the term in my choreography because of the waves of automatic movement behavior those two words produce. The term acts like a foil that makes the body interesting to notice when that language is applied. When I remember to flip the switch on the controls that situate me as Deborah and replace her with the abundant multi-faceted potentiality coming from my cellular body, I can occasionally transcend my choreographed reaction to a sensual dance. I have a trick to avoid time adrift in my habitual patterning. I "just get moving and call wherever I am" a sensual dance and notice from those instances what a sensual dance might otherwise be. The cast recognized how similarly they were trapped by my terminology. After a few weeks of practice I suggested that the sensual*

dance be performed in relation to space, especially the space between the dancer and audience. Can the audience see a dancer's perception of space as sensual?

But this was unnecessary. By its premiere the ensemble had clearly identified and let go of their entrenched sensual dance imagery and behavior. I say this declaratively because, whenever this section was reached in performance, I never again recognized it as the sensual dance, nor did I want to, because whatever was in its place was so matter-of-factly resplendent.

Dancers' notes: Holding hands begins sensual dance for me. Maybe because Amelia takes my hand very sweetly and softly. I love transforming shock into the sensual dance. It is a relief to take the inhale out of the shock so now it is more in my body rather than my breath. The sensual dance feels like an imposition, to try and work with sensuality within this Frankenstein dance. The more I let all this cycle through, the more fun it is. It is the most challenging part. I need all the questions here. How small or large is the spectrum of my seeing? The sensuality of a small area and playing within that in relation to larger space, plus my own sentimentality. A celebration of the sensuality of space and how it feeds me through the performance. It is nice to have the history of what sensuality has been and has meant to me. I feel like the sensual dance is asking something of the audience. Images of sensuality are abundant anywhere you look yet I don't want to get trapped by an image.

Specialized movement directions bring the dancers toward the audience in a uniform line except for Amelia. She remains in place singing her wordless rendition of "If I Sing to You," setting the tone for the sensual dance. Her voice aims to touch the audience. A pre-recording of Amelia's song is heard echoing her real time performance.

Catherine: slowly finds her way with her back to the audience. She does not use her arms and barely alters her passage.

Vera: other than getting downstage, she is limited to moving her head, and even that is scarce.

Juliette and Jeanine: form a cartoon-like fox-trot position. They dance a stiff side-to-side triplet, turning and moving in line with Vera, who is next to them. They bump their extended and clasped hands into Vera's chest with each turn of their dance. This disturbs Vera, who looks at them askance. They separate from the line and begin strolling, the inside arm draped behind the other's back. Strolling stage left, they then make a wide curve upstage and back toward Amelia. Their travel is in a Sunday-in-the-park kind of time.

Michelle: loosens her hair, plays with it and more imagined hair. She smiles a lot, and makes vanishing girly gestures. Her path weaves slightly while Catherine and Vera's paths are direct.

Once downstage, Michelle joins Catherine to face Amelia. Michelle taps her foot to signal Vera to begin her sensual dance. The same tap prompts Juliette and Jeanine to stop

Figure 8 **If I Sing to You.** Left to right: Jeanine Durning and
Juliette Mapp (© Sylvio Dittrich, 2008).

strolling and drop their heads. With some degree of tension
in their bodies, Michelle and Catherine advance upstage.
Every tap of their shoes has the potential to destabilize
singing Amelia, who interprets self-selected taps as blows
to her body that finally set her in motion along a zigzag
path to the downstage left corner. The recording ends
the moment Amelia abandons the place where she has
been standing since the beginning of this sequence.

> *No big deal becomes useful when too much energy or
> attention is given to a movement that by its very descrip-
> tion is impossible to do. There is almost always a part of
> every dancer I have ever worked with, including myself,
> who believes it is possible to achieve the impossible.*

Dancers' notes: I feel relieved at not having directions other than making song and enjoying the stillness of my body. Challenging to blow it out and take more liberties. I want the integrity of the song but I want the song to be anything at anytime. Hearing Amelia sing helps to resolve standing in a line. I hear her respond to everything that has occurred so far. I hear her being inside of and creating the current moment. The other dancers feel like a rolling landscape, first rolling away from and then returning to me. All the while looking through a pinhole camera. It is too fast to be sensual and too fast to create sensual between the audience and me. It is hard to travel. Today, having the duet so close took pressure off of the space between the audience and me. I like my dance because I really do not know what it is. I have this strong feeling I am doing something different from everyone. It's a feeling state which is set quickly and after that I just do as little as possible. Moving downstage feels like the baseline of a chamber orchestra. A lot happens in very short time because there is so much to notice. I am aware of the air and how our paired footsteps resolve as we go along. When we drop our heads I feel as if we are holding the space.

The other dancers separately join Amelia, traveling their own zigzags to the downstage left corner. Grope and find it and pull it out, is the movement direction performed along the zigzag. (It is also a metaphor for the creative process and the name of a dance I choreographed for four London-based dancers in 2008.) The zigzag is fed by juggling the following directions:

1. do not predetermine where onstage your switch-backs happen;
2. without hesitation, remove recognizable kinetic patterning, not by stopping or changing movement but by heightening your perception of time and space;
3. notice the perfection of the ensemble's shifting geometry;
4. read one another's movement as their music.

Lighten up reflects back on a history of dance pedagogy and training that can leave many dancers victims of what I call the look of the serious artist syndrome. It also serves as a trigger for those moments when I fall into the habit of wanting to get a movement right.

Some of the words used in the score are names I have assigned movements within the sequence of the dance. They help me formulate a basis for remembering the dance, and give feedback and coaching to the dancers. Words such as curtain, dark side, string-on-fire, grope, pull it out, music, poetry, dialogue, and freefall are not meant to illustrate or represent, even though in some cases it is very tempting. A word is sometimes a trap that becomes thrilling to evade, or a word like dialogue can force the dancer to yield to the intelligence of her cellular body.

Dancers' notes: Having to step up to grope and find it and pull it out from the song is edgy and quick and as it goes on I become more amoeba-like. It is challenging. I feel Amelia's presence in the beginning of Grope. What I do is totally based on her first moves. I get a lot of information from others' nothing and that informs mine. Interesting to surrender the energy of doing something. Being the first one and alone, I realize I am doing something. It is confusing but I go through it just the same. Subverting the arrival is different from dismantling something. I go through a lot trying to thwart personal impulses. Sometimes I just change the body part and let the instructions ride around my body so I don't narrow. If I let go of the tyranny of the cohesive self, I enjoy it. I feel like I am earning my paycheck. My nervous system runs high. Good not to do that. Challenge is to be fuzzier or less defined. The first zigzag is so hard. I am just waiting for the next one. I can take care of getting what I need in zigzag. The stillness seems to pop out of the tidal wave because I can recognize the same physical experience differently so I don't have to keep changing. Anything can happen and that is the essence of creativity. I imagine the piece in London and what it looked like. I always forget Grope . . . other words come up and I get all messed up. Hilarious that I cannot get the linear language to fit and be something. I have no idea. I think of what DH says about it being a metaphor for the creative process and it is exhilarating to continue. It is freeing to have a new perspective. "This is nothing. This is nothing." This is a relief and I am very busy. The sensation is too much but I am in the flow of the zigzag. Sometimes I see Michelle not moving and I think I could stop but I do not. I try to use the others because it is all so difficult. My problem is that it goes too fast. For the moment all movement feels reflexive. At the end of the zigzag I have the sensation that I didn't breath.

At the downstage corner, each dancer turns without turning on half-toe, traveling in a straight line diagonally upstage right to the furthest point. Here a second zig-zag path starts, contrasting sharply with the former one. The dancers move like shards of light as one or both arms and/or legs lift and lower with fast, clear, razor-like and seemingly weightless precision. When the right down-stage corner is reached, the dancers again turn without turning on half-toe, moving along a straight diagonal line upstage left, fitting themselves into a single wedge in the corner, facing stage right.

Here and gone, here and gone, here and gone is a directive I repeat aloud through many a practice session because time is passing and we all would rather it not. So we attach to a movement, often because it feels good, we like it, it is beautiful, or just challenging. We fix on what we are doing and as a consequence lose touch with what else is around us, including the audience.

Dancers' notes: I try not to drop into turning without turning because I need to navigate my path. I have the feeling of a pique turn and remember head spotting. I think of a top, when you spin it and it looks still. And even though I do not look like that that is what I am thinking about. I am trying to include my perception of the whole space. This informs me freshly plus I invite being seen because my energy can drop here. I got stuck a while back, and then remembered that there is no way to do it. I love watching everyone and how different we all are. I like turning left, however that is. The second zigzag is here and I can see the light. Oh it is going to be better soon and then my body reacts by accelerating. I am excited about the possibility of loving the zigzag – like what challenges me the most will save me. I try to be light and clear. I am trying and doing and don't know why. The zigzag is limiting, narrow, and I forget 360 degrees. I do not turn. I feel pushed. And I hate my shoes. I can't use my legs. Sometimes I feel like I am someone else. A Finnish guy with elbows. I feel like I am pretending to be light and bright and clear. But I enjoy pretending. No weight. Getting a lot from seeing others being light around me. I feel aware of being in a coda. I am aware of an escalating energy and the tightness of our geometry and it has become a collective movement. I am aware the dance is ending soon and there is a lot of work before reaching the corner. I am into dangerous razor-like lines with images of the ethereal. The switch in my perception to my cellular body frees me up and I am getting a lot from everyone. Everything is in response to what I see others doing. I hear cymbals; it feels like an anthem or an orchestra at full volume. It is neat to wind up in the corner after all of that lightness moving through space. I get to use my legs differently. I actually think light and how fast light travels, and how it moves through space like different wavelengths and different degrees of lightness. The movement at the switchbacks is powerful. I used to have Trisha in mind. I am not in the forefront of what happens. I am just inside of it. I like the sensation of being pulled along. I am surprised by the rhythm of the zigzag and turning and the organization of our arrival. I fall directly into the group with no physical cuts. I enjoy watching how differently everyone turns without turning, especially when I get to the corner first. Everyone's music rolls in towards me. I hear us out of breath and try not to drop the dance. We have worked so hard and will all go to the sauna afterwards.

After an undetermined time a single dancer leaves the standing wedge performing a blowsy march in a straight line across stage. She semi-struts without a trace of commentary in her performance. Before exiting she glances at the audience for just a moment.

Is it enough to see a dancer's intelligence at work, separate from what she/he is doing?

Blackout.

The lighting technician determines when the blackout occurs.

Dancers' notes: There is this last bit of possibility ushered into the world. It gets me out of myself to think that the lighting technician determines the end. I feel like I am in the right place. I love arriving here, working on being seen looking like I am facing one direction but not. I like seeing the blowsy march from behind. It looks so beautiful. Especially Catherine. I am always amazed at being something so amazing, about how you can do it.

If I sing to you
I would try and tell you everything I know
My song would be so still.
dh 2/2007

Figure 9 body drawing 2.

June 2008

I learn what my dances will become through the practice of very uninteresting sequences of movement material that has almost no meaning or value to me. I become the choreographer only after the practice of the performance of the sequence informs me of the unity of the dance.

February 2009

If I can maintain my perception of time and space as inspiring essentials in my experience of performance then two-thirds of my work is already happening. Attention to my whole body as my teacher in relation to the audience and the other dancers with whom I may be performing is the fundamental and final component.

What if less is more is not less?

Previously I practiced how I see in relation to the audience, without including the space between myself and them nor the space that reaches to the edges of the theater or studio. This now adds greatly to the noticeable material I can apply to my dancing.

Turn your fucking head is the single movement direction used in the practice of my work. It is meant to disrupt beliefs that what you are doing matters, whether or not you are conscious that you have this belief. In the context of my work, what matters is not what you do but how you are choosing to engage in the moment.

TYFH came like a shot out of hell as I watched myself on video. Because other people were in the room, I kept the ongoing entreaty to turn your fucking head to myself. I was dancing as if I could control all the elements of my performance if I just held my head still enough. It was painful to observe but it became a turning point in my understanding of performance, particularly in relation to my work.

The regal head is endemic to dance and theater practitioners. As artists we need to prove we are serious and responsible citizens of the world, committed to our respective art forms, who know what we are doing and want the audience to know this too. This need to assert our value in society lodges the head like a fortress, unwilling to surrender.

I began to loosen up. Rather than my head turning as a consequence of dancing, I found it more effective to arbitrarily turn my head as if in response to someone calling my name, or a book falling on the floor nearby. Coincidentally with every shift in my visual field when my head did turn, my body experienced a differentiation of physicality.

I turn my fucking head to refresh my body palette; in other words, creating or inventing movement becomes obsolete. There is an infinite source of movement material already happening in my body and by turning my fucking head, and routinely noticing how my body is changed by how I am seeing, dance is already happening. My work is to attend to its brief lifetime.

TYFH also helps keep the cellular body in the question. I am so easily absorbed by my personal experiences and in live performance this means I lose sight of the audience, other cast members, and/or the space where I am performing.

TYFH requires a willingness to surrender linear and habitual patterning in movement and thought. It forces an awareness of the constant reorganization of the body within the space where performance is happening, not where the head happens to be as a consequence of movement or choreography. It ushers in a dynamic and constructive relationship within the performance environment.

Practice is learning without thinking.

How I see relates to my perception of time passing so that my eyes become practiced at not dwelling either inwardly or outwardly. My eyes do not attach to an object in view or in mind. I am learning how to lightly dis-attach from my patterns of seeing.

The overuse of the word "detach" makes it too facile, making it lose the experience of the personal. To dis-attach requires more action on my part as a practitioner. I need to recognize where I am before I can choose to dis-attach from where I am.

When dancers learn to dis-attach from their particular strengths their transparency is visibly matchless.

The experience of seeing when I am dancing, what I imagine, think, invent, project, within the areas close, mid-range, and far, unfolds in my body, not out there.

Something lifts in the upper part of the back of my head when I include what I cannot see in my practice of seeing.

April 2009

Remember to remove your innate sequencing from the sequence of the dance's structure.

What if my bodily perception of time is that it is passing? What if as an audience member I can watch dance through this lens? I rarely, if ever, remember to see dance through this lens.

My practice of dis-attachment from the continuity of the continuity of my choreographed body reminds me that beyond my rather limited personal experiences (thank god for them!), there are endless dances waiting to be realized.

By removing your instinctive and behavioral sequencing from the structural sequence of the dance, time and space can expand forever.

No Time to Fly

Premiere: St. Mark's Church in-the-Bowery, New York,
March 25–27, 2010

Joy and sorrow in the audience
In my body
How I see
Onstage
In time passing.

Joy and sorrow in movement
Choreography
Performance
My voice
Dance
At once
Rhythm
And work.

Joy and sorrow in history
Language
Reform
At once
complexity
Fanfare
Prayer.

Four questions for the dancer

What if the question "What if where I am is what I need?" is not about what I need but an opportunity to inhabit the question "What if where I am is what I need?"?

What if dance is how I practice my relationship with my whole body at once in relationship to the space where I am dancing in relationship to each passing moment in relationship to my audience? What if the depth of this question is on the surface?

What if my choice to surrender the pattern, and it is just a pattern, of facing a single direction or fixing on a single idea, feeling, or object when I am dancing is a way of remembering to see where I am in order to surrender where I am?

What if how I see while I am dancing is a means by which movement arises without looking for it?

Three reminders for my practice

Remove my sequencing from the sequence of movement directions.

Remove hesitation and reconsideration.

A word or short phrase in CAPS is a warning to avoid my automatic response to be creative or to fall into habitual behavior regarding the words I use. Instead, I immediately dis-attach[7] from those impulses by noticing

---

[7] My use of the word "dis-attach" instead of "detach": to detach has become a generalized concept that, at this time, often loses the experience of the personal. To dis-attach requires more action on my part as a practitioner. I need to recognize where I am before I can choose to dis-attach from where I am.

the whole body at once as my teacher, thus assuming the cellular intelligence of my body.

I enter the stage area as the last few audience members take their seats, performing instances of Fred Astaire and Ginger Rogers that contributed to shaping my body memory. I am not imitating or representing but relying on my awareness of being choreographed by images of them since early childhood. During FRED AND GINGER I also decide where my entrance into *No Time to Fly* will be and what direction I will travel in relation to the audience and where that path will end. I then step to the side of the stage, which I just designated as my entrance site, and the light fades.

The moment the light returns I begin walking in a stride and style not mine, as foreign as a foreign accent, recognizable but odd. The path is a singular broad curve that ends in a slightly accelerated little curl, leaving me facing the portal through which I stepped on stage.

Note: Nothing about my performance ends at the end of the curl.

Note: I attend to the exactness of the single broad curve so that when I face my entrance site it is as if I complete the stringing of an archer's bow.

Note: I deliberately create this space within a space, separating me from the audience.

I am held by an imagined cord linking me to the portal.

An ancient voice quietly advises me to remember the audience as well as the space beyond my tightly contained space.

Note: The ancient voice is me from 10,000 years ago or from 10,000 years in the future, bringing that possibility into the present.

In response to the guidance received, I select the right moment to break the string and notice at once how the inclusion of the theater and my audience enlarges my dancing. It is like a real opening, and I begin again.

Note: My choice to perform this material requires catastrophic acts of perception. I associate catastrophic with images of great loss. The magnitude and reoccurrence of choreographed behavior that I need to first recognize and then dis-attach from, again and again, is a personal loss of tremendous proportion.

My body is still while JOY AND SORROW wash across my face like a stream of instances. When not streaming, my face may briefly return to normalcy, or it may sustain a single reflection of joy/sorrow for longer moments.

Note: I am not limited to my personal experience of joy and sorrow. It is a relief to know that it is in and about the audience, this theater, and the world beyond its doors.

Note: As I perform, I try to remove my tendency to embody the images I use to describe the movement material.

I sing a WORDLESS SONG that arises from and combines joy and sorrow into a single melody that resonates through my bones. Barely suppressing a sense of personal history, my face reflects the transience of JOY AND SORROW.

Note: I hear the song as my voice leaves my body. I am intentionally unguarded because I rarely allow myself to partake in unprotected experiences.

Note: I am not translating the written language into movement, i.e., joy and sorrow. I actually aspire toward a bodily speechlessness by noticing my visual field, which includes what I can and cannot see, as well as minute associative instances that rise spontaneously.

Note: I understand that joy and sorrow are always present. I do not have to instigate them.

The song's duration is determined by how much time is required for the WORDLESS SONG to impress itself on my body and the audience's memory. Its phrasing can expand and contract.

Note: Singing a song of joy and sorrow is a challengingly simple way for me to engage my perception of space and time.

I attach rhythmic movement to the song, my dancing obviously influenced by my singing. I establish this continuity of relationship before using it to navigate a slightly complex path to the edge of the stage.

Note: I strongly maintain the role of the choreographer, overseeing the particularity of the path I travel and making spatial choices without becoming too artistic.

Partway, my audible singing disappears, yet the dancing adheres to its reliance on the now unheard rhythm of the song.

And finally my dance shifts outside of the prevailing memory of the song, and I move across stage in a straight line while erasing my destination.

Note: While dancing I make an effort not to hesitate. Learned behavior suggests I slow down or listen more in order to get things right. That is a belief that limits my dance.

At the edge of the stage, I have a one-minute allotment to turn in place a single time without moving slowly or continuously. I sing snippets of the WORDLESS SONG on two or three occasions during the turn.

Note: My head is free to look down or away or to turn. It is not fixed.

If the sparsely singing turn is like a lock unlocking, then WORK is my deliverance into space after one minute.

Note: I accept any movement that arises spontaneously and call it WORK.

WORK is a variation on two spontaneous movements lasting two seconds each and used to cross stage one time. Because of the banality of choreography, WORK is also how I manage the choreographic tools I need to maintain both my interest and that of the audience. Those tools are the perception of my movement as music, my perception of space, the use of stillness and duration, and the perception of joy and sorrow to deepen my practice of performance.

Note: During WORK it is helpful to get an aerial view of where and how I am using the stage area.

Note: There is no repetition in live performance.

Note: WORK comes easily. Maybe it is because of what is required to survive as a dancer in contemporary western culture. It can be difficult to dis-attach from the habitual physical response to what "work" looks like: i.e., striving, reaching, pushing, dragging, busying, flailing, hauling.

Note: I neither hurry nor linger.

COMPLEXITY arises. I play with how I perceive time and how I perceive space rather than creating complex body movement. FREEDOM FROM COMPLEXITY is as abstruse, yet here I am, two alternating occurrences weaving back and forth several times. The duration for each of the two parts is choreographically challenging.

Note: The movement is not difficult just because I use the words COMPLEXITY, havoc, abstruse, choreographically challenging. And FREEDOM FROM COMPLEXITY does not necessarily require flowing movement.

Note: If I can manage my perception of time and space to inform my body, then I do not have to think about what movement to do next. What I mean by my perception of time is that it is passing. And what I mean by my perception of space is that I include it in my dancing so that I am not seduced by the intelligence, past experiences, patterns, limitations, and/or sensuality of my moving body.

I perform market, a contemporary market, A MALL. Without creating A MALL I notice it wherever I am.

Note: I attend to my perception of space and time in order to distract myself from predetermining the outcome of this choreographic direction. It is an effort to refrain from

Figure 10 **No Time to Fly**. solo adaptation by Ros Warby (© Rino
Pizzi, 2012).

creating a literal mall. Instead, copious instances of A
MALL *appear and disappear as I dance.*

A single OBJECT reveals itself in a mall. I perform several views of OBJECT for the benefit of the audience. A
MALL and OBJECT alternate their appearances.

Note: I do not create OBJECT. *I learn its attributes from
my body and actually take pleasure in identifying the
object for myself in each performance.*

Note: I remember to notice that my whole body is producing unimaginable instances of specificity.

I start spinning, not literally but as a part of an onstage counterclockwise spinning vortex that only I perceive. I am a speck, a dot, a flake, endlessly spiraling toward center stage, and absolutely no one can possibly identify me as such.

Note: The movement may change, but the choreography itself does not change.

At center stage I reverse direction and turn in place while lifting my arms incrementally, to signify the construction and architecture of A HOLY SITE. At the same time my shoes lightly tap the floor under me as if to imply the sporadic thwacks of a hammer striking in the distance.

Note: I am A HOLY SITE and to perform as such requires the catastrophic loss of how I otherwise perceive myself.

A HOLY SITE is completed the moment my hands or fingertips touch overhead. I open my mouth and hear A HOLY SONG rise up out of me.

Note: I call what I hear A HOLY SONG and notice the feedback from my whole body as it yields to that direction.

Unable to sustain itself, A HOLY SITE collapses. My hands, still touching, drop before my eyes. I contemplate the symbolism of the gestural demise.

Resourcing whatever bits of prior exposure to a fake American Indian ritual dance, primarily Hollywood westerns, I discharge those bits as best as I can while rhythmlessly bouncing to beating drums that only I can hear.

My fake American Indian ritual collapses. I rebuild A HOLY SITE, using the sound of my tapping feet to symbolize the sound of distant hammering. I travel in fading light.

Light returns and I am tiptoeing, not wanting to disrupt the space already created – a task I hold in high regard. I experience space parting, with little disturbance, hoping that the audience will see this too, before arriving somewhere that is not center stage. My actions are obvious.

When I imagine the stage is still, a return to the fake American Indian ritual dance occurs. I may be the only person in the world to realize this, yet, punctuated by beating drums that only I can hear, I bounce rhythmlessly.

I lift and point my right index finger in the air and, speaking with an accent, say, "Strictly speaking I believe I have never been anywhere" (Beckett, 2000: p. 25).

With my finger still in the air, I leave time for the Beckett quote[8] to sink in.

Note: The quote's impact on my body is mind-boggling.

---

[8]This is the fourth consecutive time that this simple sentence, "Strictly speaking I believe I have never been anywhere," has been appropriated into my choreography. It has been spoken in *I'll Crane for You*, *Up Until Now*, and *Market*.

My right hand lowers as I hum an exaggerated departure from the tune "Oh, they don't wear pants in the sunny side of France. But they do wear grass, to cover up their ass." I may not even hum or I stop and start. My perception of joy and sorrow guides the singing. The lifetime of my singing is how long it takes for my hand to lower while crossing the stage without anyone knowing. My standard for "lower" is my own.

Note: My hand can be a trap. I do not fixate on it – deliberately hiding its function in determining my movement.

I am unquantifiable instances of a 5,000-YEAR-OLD MARKETPLACE before sunrise, while it is still dark and quiet. I depend on the image at first, and then I get rid of it. This is not a narrative. My hand occasionally thrums my body for sound, or I make short intermittent sounds that are barely audible.

Note: It is an effort to refrain from creating a 5,000-YEAR-OLD MARKETPLACE. *Copious instances of predawn marketplaces live and die spontaneously in my cellular memory. It is all I need.*

It is the same for a single item, such as a particular utensil, tool, or ornament – an ANCIENT OBJECT in a 5,000-YEAR-OLD MARKETPLACE. There is no name for the item. I provide several views of an ANCIENT OBJECT for the audience.

I perform COUNTERINTUITIVE TRAVEL somewhere at the edge of the space, occasionally producing a CRANKY sound.

Note: COUNTERINTUITIVE TRAVEL *reflects possibility, not opinion, psychology, or effort.*

Note: I do not become cranky. CRANKY *describes the sound of my voice.*

I MEND the field.

Note: Accepting any movement, I call it MEND. *It is a lot of work to not automatically produce comforting arm or hand movements or behave like a mother hen.*

I build a road with my feet used to smooth and design its surface. My work is clear and evident, without rest. I whisper a rhythmic sound, like an engine, to create a counterpart to the work of building the road. My arms, held out from my body, shape the engine.

Note: I strongly maintain the role of the choreographer, overseeing the design element of the road. I think of the road's surface as a mosaic, without getting too artistic.

I turn and turn and turn, as many times as I remain interested in turning on this big new road, bringing separate parts together in a whirling whole that becomes A HOLY SITE near the center of the stage. The turning is happening in my perception of the whole stage, and my body is just a part of it.

My arms are above my head, and they function as the architecture of the temple, shrine, church, mosque, etc. My hands, like antenna, immediately draw A HOLY SONG down through A HOLY SITE and out through my mouth. It does not have to be anything other than holy – holy being different for everyone.

I sing until a single abrupt sound causes my collapse and I am poised like a mound of rubble. Holding my body still, I step toward the audience to offer them several views of the former HOLY SITE.

I rebuild the road in just a few steps, using my feet as before. At center stage, my arms again lift above my head in increments, to symbolize the building of a new HOLY SITE. As soon as my hands are overhead A HOLY SONG returns.

A second abrupt fall with a single abrupt sound destroys the HOLY SITE again, turning it back into rubble.

My ancient self's voice guides me back to a standing position. Everything seems in order. I am standing straight, except that I am facing away from the audience. Final encouragement received from my ancient self has me turn to face the audience once more.

Pause.

My face streams with JOY AND SORROW.

> *Note:* Three novels by the author Jim Crace – *Quarantine*, *Gift of Stones*, and *Pesthouse* – significantly inspired the early development of **No Time to Fly**. His descriptions of pre- or post-societal communities and landscapes felt bizarrely familiar, revealing a sensual vocabulary I did not know I could access.

August 2009

The questions relegated to the cellular body are akin to having millions of balls in the air at once. It is clearly impossible and it requires practice.

October 2009

If I really want to celebrate the ephemeral nature of dance then I must learn to see and respect time passing. It seems to me that so much of dance still struggles against this stunning attribute of the form.

In my work there is **no time** for anything to happen, or, to quote Beckett, "Strictly speaking I believe I have never been anywhere."

April 2010

Calvino: "Whenever humanity seems condemned to heaviness, I think I should fly like Perseus into a different space. I don't mean escaping into dreams or into the irrational. I mean that I have to change my approach, look at the world from a different perspective [my body's intelligence] with different logic and with fresh methods of cognition and verification. . . . my working method has more often than not involved the subtraction of weight" (Calvino, 1988: p. 7).

What if *dance is how and where you practice relationship* with your whole body at once in relationship to the space where you are dancing in relationship to each passing moment in relationship to your audience? What if the depth of this question is on the surface?

What if your choice to surrender the pattern, and it is just a pattern, of facing a single direction or fixing on a singularly coherent idea, feeling, or object when you are dancing is a way to remember to see where you are in order to surrender where you are?

What if how you see while you are dancing is a means by which movement arises without looking for it?

January 2011

There is no time to identify what you see, yet you have to see in order to dis-attach from what you see. What is tricky is the simultaneous experience of seeing and dis-attaching from *what* you see. This, then, becomes how you see.

August 2012

In order to get the most from my work, you will want to notice and redirect your reliance on your physical body and what it can *do*. Redirecting this dependence requires an unselfish regard for your whole body at once as a cogent medium for indefinable specificity. You are thus positioned to learn without thinking.

What if the question "What if where I am is what I need?" is not about what you need but an opportunity to inhabit the question "What if where I am is what I need?"?

What if how you see while you are dancing, including what you imagine, invent, project, can and cannot see in a prescribed area near, mid-range, and far, at any given moment, is a means by which movement arises without looking for it? What if how you see happens here in your body and not out there? What if how you see is the subject of your experience instead of what you see being an object in your experience?

Richmond Hall (2012)

this empty space
a song
an ocean
a figure moves
an ocean
the figure a sea
weaving her destiny
repeatedly
dh, 2012

Richmond Hall was a former grocery store in Houston, TX. The Menil Foundation acquired the building in 1985 and in 1996 it became the site for a permanent Dan Flavin installation. Each of my visits to the museum furthered a desire to perform in Flavin's pastel world just as it was. In 2012, in conjunction with the exhibition *Silence*, Toby Kamps, curator of new and contemporary art at the Menil Collection, invited me to choreograph a twenty-minute site-specific work for Richmond Hall, which also became the title of the dance. I performed a solo with six local dancers who each became a guide for one of six quickly determined waiting audience members. Their invitation was "be with, beside, behind, or near me. I am taking you into the dance." The audience member followed their respective guide, who indicated where to loosely gather in relation to the space, to the other independently traveling or standing groups, and to my solo. The guide would determine when the group moved to another site several times during the dance. The spatial parameters for my solo allowed me to determine where I was in relation to the physical space and to the six ad hoc groups, sometimes choosing

Figure 11 **Richmond Hall** (© Lynn Lane, 2012).

to dance behind one group who would then become
the background for a group standing in front of me. I
could be viewed from near and far and at times move
within or through a standing arrangement of people as I
performed **Richmond Hall** in Richmond Hall.

Dance

> *this empty stage*
> *an ocean*
> *dh*

Things grow in it, not on it. No grass, no trees
bending and waving as it moves. It rises and falls
like the chest of a breathing animal. To swim in it
is to immerse in its power, either to fight it
if that is the word for thrashing and kicking across
its unfeeling surface, or to ride on it, gliding and stroking,
to let it carry you, consenting to its direction.
Even when violent storms whip its surface
like water shaken in a jar, only a short way down
and further down, its enormous heart beats calmly,
its breaths are even and deep and the art
of only one dancer is needed to cram
within this stage the perilous ocean undiminished.

Barry Goldensohn (2013)

May 2013

My Body, the Archive

"Can I transmit a dance to a group of dancers who I
do not know, based solely on the language I have been

crafting for forty-five years?" This seemed like a logical development in my working process.

I had actually come to *believe* that I had created a spoken/written language that could convey how to perform my work, despite my suspicions about belief. As a matter of fact, one of my recurring coaching themes is "You do not have to believe that there is a truth to the question. Just move the question from your head down through your whole body and notice how the sensual impact from the question alters you."

Based on the affinity to my language that seems to have inspired many dancers, including students and professionals, I had come to *believe* that if dancers attend to my questions, using them as tools to engage their awareness in the practice of my work, then they would be prepared to perform my choreography. This *belief* was a solution to participating in a project curated by Ralph Lemon, titled *some sweet day*, at the Museum of Modern Art (MoMA) in New York City in Fall 2012. Other commitments already in place prevented me from spending any serious time in New York to work with the cast of twenty-two dancers, ten of whom I had never met and twelve of whom I had worked with only briefly in the past. In order to choreograph **Blues** I had to take a chance that a method was in place.

This method, not exclusive to me, consisted of writing performance and choreographic directions to the cast, asking them for feedback, to respond with questions, thoughts, or issues. This was all conducted by email and took place over nine months leading up to the public performances at MoMA. It was a perfect opportunity to test my *belief* that a method was in place to transmit my work through a language that had been tested, had failed, and was redefined, retested, and refined through coaching and directing hundreds of performers, both students and professionals, since 1970.

I *believed* I could do without the intimate and concentrated process that has served my choreography and the dancers with whom I have worked for the last forty-five years. That *belief* felt real because that is how *belief* works. It is how and why we build religions, skyscrapers, philosophies, prophecies, laws – you name it – and how and why we destroy them. I *believed* I had achieved and articulated a method for the transmission of my work through language.

The dance I choreographed for MoMA was the result of my *belief* that writing might substitute for what actually inspires language – the experience, depth, tone, trust, and absence of fear that drive my teaching and practice. I learned that the transmission of my dances needs my thorough and personal intervention as a choreographer, dancer, teacher, coach, and director. *Blues* was a bitter/sweet reminder that there is no method to convey my work because my work is a practice. That is all. It is a practice for the choreographer, the dancer, and the audience.

No matter how detailed or broad my language, between the written directions and the dancer, unforeseen circumstances and interpretations emerge that cannot be accounted for because my choreographic language deliberately and often omits specifying movement or time and/or space. Not enough sleep, a sudden meaning that a movement provokes, another war, the presence of an audience and the adrenalin that produces, an unpaid bill, a flood, a costume choice are examples of unaccountable situations. As reflected in past performances of my work, following a period of teaching and coaching and months of practice, those unknowable conditions can be sidestepped in favor of the immersive and elevating experience possible through the practice of performance.

How completely inane my language must sound to anyone not familiar with my working process. Most of the dances I choreographed in the last fifteen years were followed with a written score based solely on my daily practice of the performance of that dance. At the start of transmitting that dance to others, the prose score was read aloud. At the conclusion of the reading, practically everyone would agree that no one understood anything about the dance or how it could possibly be realized. After the dancers learned the sequence of movement directions that shape the dance, and my coaching was under way, and the tools for performing the material were tested, we would read the score again. Suddenly the text would come to life, but only through the experience of the language as it was physically embodied by each individual dancer.

My body, the archive, will not be archived.

my choreographed body / *a solo dance for an intimate setting (2014)*

For as long as I can remember I struggled with whether the questions that are applied in the performance of my work be included in printed program notes. My dances would not exist without them. The conflict about identifying the questions in the program is that I do not want audiences to be looking for what might either satisfy or not satisfy their beliefs about what they are seeing.

I come out of the closet in *my choreographed body*. All choreographed material that can otherwise prevent audiences from immediate access to my practice of performance is eliminated. I perform without

1. a structural sequence that requires my demolition of its edifice;
2. the choreographed layering of language that I previously packed into the fleetingness of performance.

my choreographed body does include the strategies I have adopted in order to change, tinker with, bypass, yield to, and play with the choreography of my learned behavior as it unfolds in my dancing.

What if I presume I am served by how I see? The question requires that I selectively interact with the world as an unknown resource for my practice of dance. "I" is mutually my whole body at once, the zillion-celled body, and Deborah conceiving of herself as such.

I need to consistently balance, *to presume*, *to be served*, and *to see* in order for **my choreographed body** to function without glitches, and there are glitches.

To presume happens faster than seeing. The authority and audacity it requires makes me laugh.

From a very early age I was taught that to presume was bad behavior. It is the opposite of what I respect most in other people.

It is willful and venturesome and I cannot be passive.

To presume is difficult for me to maintain.

I need courage to permit myself to be served. As a phrase, "I am served" reads as selfish and aggrandizing. This is why the question begins with "what if I presume . . . " and ends with "how I see."

To presume I am being served is not familiar to me, yet the authorship I experience with it in the studio instantaneously invigorates my dancing.

"What if I presume I am being served by how I see?" stirs movement that changes my cellular body. I move with feelings of gratitude that arise from the question. How I see helps prevent my dwelling on the pleasure of being served and the overconfident pitfall in presuming. The sensuality of gratitude is not modified as my movement changes.

How I choose to see includes areas near, mid-range and far, including the audience. The entire space in which I am dancing becomes a resource for **my choreographed body**.

I am not seeing or imagining things, yet the space is not empty. I could call it a continuation of the sky.

The linear structure of the question becomes a self-perpetuating loop of possibility.

my choreographed body is how I see while dancing.

Epilogue

figure a sea using the sky

Figure a Sea is the title of a commissioned work for Sweden's Cullberg Ballet that premieres September 25, 2015, in Stockholm. This book's title, *Using the Sky: a dance,* was inspired by my dream described in the book's preface:

> February 20, 2013
>
> I am among friends. It is evening and the lake is dark and still. There is a red circular life buoy floating some distance from shore. Drifting on my back, cradled by the buoy, I realize my mind is in a thousand places so I look up at the sky. At first I see only blackness. Soon enough shades of pale amber light reveal layers of shifting and billowing clouds that force my breath to rise. Then I begin to wonder how far I have drifted. Trying to twist around to see land I fear capsizing. I take a moment to decide not to worry, and turn back to the sky.

Swimming on my back is how I exercise outdoors; thus the sky has become a body of material to notice, especially when there are no clouds, as is often the case where

I live. Fairly recently, while I was backstroking, a field of nuanced atmospheric activity came into focus through my application of the question "What if I presume I am served by how I see?" Was I seeing things because of the question, or was it an actual visible condition I never noticed before? After a few days I associated what I was seeing as a continuation of the sky, and I have been relying on that now pervasive reality to promote a sense of interconnectedness with all there is when I dance.

The resulting convergence from my side-by-side positioning of the two titles, figure a sea using the sky, created an instantaneous and visceral understanding of how the universe works, and suddenly the bottom fell out of my practice. I am participating in a process that is already happening. That process exists without me or I can choose to enter it. It is an experience beyond belief. I do not have to go somewhere to acknowledge it. There is no beginning or end to any movement I am doing.

I seem to have stumbled into a meditation. In other words, I am without the mediation of questions to help me maintain an actual interest in dancing, alone or with other dancers and/or with an audience, from one moment to the next, in any given venue. The difference between using the question or not is enormous. There is a kind of busyness I now see in my practice, perhaps because of the work it takes to remain interested in noticing change. That busyness is gone in this new dance, and its power to evoke gratitude is unstoppable.

Even now "using the sky" is too definitive.

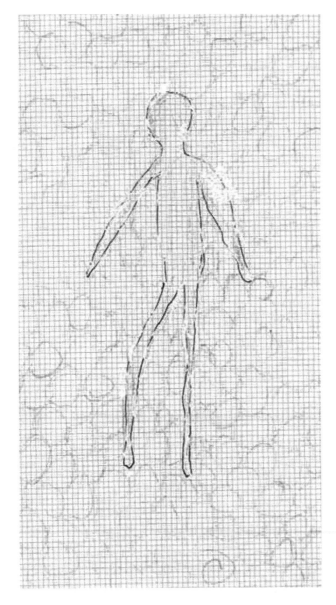

Figure 12 body drawing 3.

Dances choreographed from 2000
to the present

September 2000	***Single Duet*** (duet with Mikhail Baryshnikov)
	McCarter Theatre, Princeton, New Jersey
September 2000	***Whizz*** (White Oak Dance Project, ensemble)
	McCarter Theatre, Princeton, New Jersey
November 2001	***Music*** (solo)
	University of Texas, Austin, Texas
January 2003	***o beautiful*** (solo)
	Skidmore College Dance Theater, NY
May 2003	***Sweetening the Abstract*** (group)
	Art Museum of South Texas, Corpus Christi, TX
July 2003	***Beauty*** (solo)
	Greenwich Dance Agency, London, England
February 2004	***The Match*** (quartet)
	Danspace Project, NYC
March 2004	***A Lecture on the Performance of Beauty*** (solo)
	Movement Research at Judson Church, NYC
June 2005	***The Ridge*** (solo)
	Montpellier Danse Festival, France
January 2006	***"O, O"*** (quintet, New York cast)
	Danspace Project, New York

May 2006	*My Country Music* (ensemble)
	Grand Theater d'Angers, France
June 2006	*"O, O"* (sextet, French cast)
	Les Subsistances, Lyon, France
September 2006	*Mountain* (trio)
	Time Based Arts Festival, Portland, Oregon
November 2006	*Room* (solo)
	Marseille Objectif Danse, France
October 2007	*Go* (solo)
	Toronto Dance Theatre, Toronto, Canada
January 2008	*Grope and Find It and Pull It Out* (quartet)
	Laban Center, London, England
April 2008	*If I Sing to You* (sextet)
	Festpielhaus Hellerau, Dresden, Germany
July 2008	*Found Music* (duet)
	Crowley Theater, Marfa, Texas
January 2009	*Up Until Now* (ensemble)
	Toronto Dance Theatre, Canada
March 2010	*No Time To Fly* (solo)
	Danspace Project, New York, New York
April 2010	*Breaking the Chord* (ensemble)
	Springdance Festival, The Netherlands
August 2010	*Lightening* (septet)
	Helsinki Arts Festival, Finland
June 2011	*Indivisibilities* (duet co-choreographed with Laurent Pichaud)
	Montpellier Danse Festival, France

September 2011	*A Lost Opera* (trio)
	Project Arts Centre, Dublin, Ireland
October 2011	*As Holy Sites Go* (trio)
	Frankfurt LAB, Frankfurt am Main, Germany
October 2012	*Richmond Hall* (solo with group)
	Richmond Hall, Houston, Texas
October 2012	*Blues* (ensemble)
	Museum of Modern Art, New York
December 2012	*As Holy Sites Go/duet*
	Danspace Project, New York
September 2015	*Figure a Sea* (Cullberg Ballet, ensemble)
	Dansens Hus, Stockholm, Sweden

Solos choreographed for the Solo Performance Commissioning Project

The SPCP took place at Whidbey Island Center for the Arts, Whidbey Island, WA, from 1998 to 2002. From 2004 through 2012 the SPCP was in residence in Universal Hall, at the Findhorn Community Foundation, Findhorn, Scotland.

August 1998	*The Other Side of O*
August 1999	*Fire*
August 2000	*Boom Boom Boom*
August 2001	*Music*
August 2002	*o beautiful*
August 2004	*The Ridge*

August 2005	*Room*
August 2006	*News*
August 2007	*The Runner*
August 2008	*I'll Crane for You*
August 2009	*At Once*
August 2010	*Art and Life*
August 2011	*I Think Not*
August 2012	*Dynamic*

Solo performance projects commissioned by individual dance presenters

August 2004	*The North Door*, commissioned by Zodiak, Center for New Dance, Helsinki, Finland
April 2009	*Market*, commissioned by Stiftelsen Dansens Hus, The House of Dance Foundation, Stockholm, Sweden
March 2010	*In the Dark*, commissioned by Dancehouse Inc., Critical Path, STRUT dance, and Bundanon Trust, Australia
March 2011	*Conquest*, commissioned by Serralves Foundation, Porto, Portugal
May/June 2012	*this empty stage an ocean*, commissioned by Cullberg Ballet, Stockholm, Sweden

References

Bachelard, Gaston, *The Poetics of Space*, Beacon Press, reprint, Boston 1994.

Becket, Samuel, *First Love and Other Novellas*, Penguin Books, London, 2000.

Calvino, Italo, *Six Memos for the Next Millennium*, Harvard University Press, Cambridge, 1988.

Goldensohn, Barry, "Dance," in *The Hundred Yard Dash Man: New and Selected Poems*, Fomite Press, Burlington, VT, 2013.